AMERICAN HISTORY

VOLUME IV: THE NORTHERN COLONIES

JACOB ABBOTT

SANDYCROFT PUBLISHING

American History Vol. IV: The Northern Colonies

By Jacob Abbott

First published 1862

This edition ©2017

Sandycroft Publishing

http://sandycroftpublishing.com

CONTENTS

CHAPTER IV
LANDING AT PLYMOUTH

CHAPTER V
FIRST WINTER AT PLYMOUTH

CHAPTER VI
MASSASOIT AND THE INDIANS

CHAPTER VII
Massachusetts Bay

CHAPTER VIII
The Dutch on the Hudson

CHAPTER IX
The Conquest of New Netherland

CHAPTER X
GROWTH AND EXTENSION OF THE COLONIES

LIST OF ENGRAVINGS

PREFACE

It is the design of this work to narrate, in a clear, simple, and intelligible manner, the leading events connected with the history of our country, from the earliest periods, down, as nearly as practicable, to the present time. The several volumes will be illustrated with all necessary maps and with numerous engravings, and the work is intended to comprise in a distinct and connected narrative, all that is essential for the general reader to understand in respect to the subject of it, while for those who have time for more extended studies, it may serve as an introduction to other and more copious sources of information.

The author hopes also that the work may be found useful to the young, in awakening in their minds an interest in the history of their country, and a desire for further instruction in respect to it. While it is doubtless true that such a subject can be really grasped only by minds in some degree mature, still the author believes that many young persons, especially such as are intelligent and thoughtful in disposition and character, may derive both entertainment and instruction from a perusal of these pages.

The settlers.

THE NORTHERN COLONIES

CHAPTER I
GOSNOLD

THE TWENTY-SECOND OF DECEMBER

The first permanent settlement that was made in the northern portion of the American territory dates from the landing of the Pilgrims, as they are called, in 1620. The day of the landing is considered to be the twenty-second of December. This day is accordingly at the present time quite extensively celebrated, among the northern states, as a very important anniversary. Indeed, the twenty-second of December, 1620, marks a great era in the history of the American continent.

UNSETTLED CONDITION OF EUROPE IN THE SIXTEENTH CENTURY

The settlement made by the Pilgrims was by no means the first that was attempted, though it was the first that was successful. A great many different expeditions were fitted out for America in the fifteenth and sixteenth centuries, by adventurous people. Indeed, Europe was full of adventurous people in those days, who evinced a degree of enterprise and daring in the voyages which they undertook to explore the shores of the new world, which seems to us at this day quite marvelous. It is true that the middle and lower classes in England, Spain, and Portugal, and in other countries in Europe, had very little reason to love their homes, and to wish to remain in them. Whether they remained at home or went away they were destined to lives of hardship and suffering. The institutions under which they lived bore very heavily upon them, and subjected them to constant

1

caprice and ill-treatment, and sometimes to cruel oppression, on the part of the nobles and the princes who ruled the land. Civil wars too were continually breaking out, and political and religious persecutions of all kinds pressed heavily upon those who were opposed to the sect or the party that was for the time being in power, so that the condition of the people at home was not by any means calculated to make them contented and happy.

Ideas in Respect to America

On the other hand most extravagant ideas prevailed in respect to the wealth and the wonders of America. For a long time America was confounded with India, and the people of those times seem to have formed their conceptions of India from the stories of the Arabian Nights. They thought the riches of that country, in gold, and silver, and gems, and silks, and spices, and perfumes, were boundless. All that was necessary was for them to find their way to those marvelous realms, with vessels in which they could bring portions of this wealth away.

When Columbus set off on his voyages of discovery, it was to the Indies that he thought he was going, and when he discovered the land he thought it was the western shores of the Indies that he saw. He called the land the West Indies, and the people Indians, which names they, both the country and the people, have retained to this day.

And long afterward, when it became known that the new world was very far from the ancient Indies, the most marvelous tales were told in Europe of the wealth of the newly discovered continent, and great numbers of expeditions were fitted out, from time to time, in different countries, some merely to visit the new lands in hopes of procuring treasure, and others with a view of making permanent settlements in them. We have given accounts of several of these expeditions, which went to the more southern portions of the continent, in the previous volumes of this series. We propose now to give an account of one of them, as a specimen of the rest, which was sent to the northern portion. The leader of the enterprise was a famous navigator of those days named Bartholomew Gosnold.

The Expedition Organized

By what has been said in respect to the unsettled and insecure condition of the people of Europe in those days, it is not meant that any great portion of them were made willing to embark in perilous enterprises and adventures, but only that such a number were driven by their misery into desperation, as to render such expeditions possible. It was however, after all, very difficult to secure the money and the men that were necessary. Gosnold found it not easy to obtain sufficient funds, nor to make up his company and his crew. The utmost that he could do was to provide means for purchasing an old and very small vessel—a bark—called the *Concord*. Then he found it difficult to procure men to navigate the bark. He at last engaged eight, but many of them were inexperienced sailors, and even if they had been good men, the number was too small. A ship's crew is divided at sea into two watches, one half being on duty at a time. This division would give Captain Gosnold only four men for the ordinary working of the ship, with the power of calling upon the other four in time of special danger, or in case of a storm. This was altogether too small a force for such a purpose.

Besides these eight sailors there were twelve men who went out with the expedition in the capacity of trading adventurers, with the intention of returning with the bark, and bringing home with them commodities of some sort which they were to procure of the natives in exchange for the merchandise which they carried out. There were also twelve more who were to remain and settle in the country, in case they should find a pleasant and fertile territory where they could live. This made up the whole number on board the bark to thirty-two.

The Voyage

The bark sailed from Falmouth in England, on the 25th of March, 1602, and those on board must have seen the shores of their native land disappear in the horizon, with many misgivings, and with much anxiety and fear. The voyage would necessarily be very long, and they were obliged to make it longer on account of the weakness of the vessel, which they knew very well would not bear any heavy strain from the winds and seas. Besides, the number of seamen was so small that it was unsafe to carry much sail in ordinary weather, since there was not nautical force enough on board to furl the sails promptly in case of any sudden change. A sudden gust of wind may come up at any time at sea so rapidly, that men are required at every sail, to take them all in together, or at least within a very brief space of time, for if they are not taken in before the squall strikes the ship she is in imminent danger of being capsized.

The bark went slowly on, driven to and fro by contrary winds, but still all the time working gradually toward the west, until about the middle of April—which was about three weeks after leaving port—and then land came in sight. The land was one of the Azores, a group of islands about midway of the Atlantic.

The company on board the bark watched this island from the deck, as long as it continued in sight, but the expedition did not land upon it. They went on, steering still to the westward. In about ten days afterward they began to observe a remarkable change in the appearance of the water. It turned to a yellow color, and they thought they were approaching land. So they sounded but they could find no bottom. They took up some of the water in a bucket, and though it looked very yellow on the sea, yet the small quantity in the bucket appeared precisely the same, as far as they could perceive, both in taste and color, as the sea water did in other parts of the ocean, where its color is a deep blue.

It is probable that it was the Gulf Stream that they were in, and that the sediment which the water contained was sufficient to affect the color when a great depth of it was seen, though it produced no visible change in the case of a small quantity, such as could be taken up in a bucket.

Still they went on. A fortnight more passed away, which brought the date to the seventh of May, and then they began to see birds in great numbers. This was an infallible sign that they were drawing near the land. The birds appeared not only in great numbers, but in great variety. There were "pigeons, petrels, coots, hagbuts, penguins, mews, gannets, cormorants and gulls, with many else in our English tongue of no name." Seeing all these birds, and thinking that the land was near, they sounded and found bottom in seventy fathoms, which is over four hundred feet. Two days afterward they sounded again and found twenty-two fathoms, which was only a little more than one hundred and twenty feet. On the bottom of the lead with which seamen sound in such cases as this, there is usually a small cavity with something adhesive in the end of it, and this brings up a portion of the sand or mud from the bottom. In this case the lead brought up sand and little shining stones, which made the trading men on board the bark think that they were coming to a land of jewels and gold.

THE LAND

They went on some days longer, watching everything all around them, and sounding very often, until at length they began to meet with floating weeds, and pieces of wood, and a day or two after this they came in sight of land.

The first view which they had of the land was early in the morning, a little after sunrise. They saw a rock rising out of the water at some distance from the shore. The shore itself was low, and bordered by a white sandy beach, with a range of hummocks of sand beyond them, along the line of the coast. Further inland the country seemed well wooded. It was a pleasant spring morning, and the whole aspect of the scene was charming to men who had now been for so many weeks tossing about in so frail a bark over the wild and stormy ocean.

VISIT FROM THE INDIANS

While the company on board the vessel were gazing intently at the shore, suddenly there appeared, coming out from the land, a good sized boat, having altogether the appearance of a Portuguese shallop, such as are built and used along the shores of the Bay of Biscay. At first they supposed that this must be some European boat, and that the people on board were Europeans, who had in some way been left on these shores. But as the shallop drew near they found that it was filled with savages. And yet the boat had a mast and a sail, and when subsequently it came alongside, it was found that the savages had an anchor on board—or rather a *grapple,* such as is used to serve the purpose of an anchor in boats of this class—and a copper kettle; and some other things, that were indubitably the products of civilization.

While Captain Gosnold and the people on board the bark were wondering what all this could mean, the boat came on until it was within call, and then one of the savages, who seemed to be the commander of the party, rose in the boat and hailed the bark. Captain Gosnold answered. Then the savage made signs of peace. There had been so many vessels from Europe on these shores—for it was now more than a hundred years since America was first discovered—and there had been so much intercourse of one kind and another with the tribes upon the coast, that quite a good understanding had been arrived at with the natives in respect to the more simple and obvious ideas which could be communicated by signs.

The savage chieftain, having received a favorable response to his signals from Captain Gosnold, proceeded to make a long and formal speech, standing in his boat all the time and addressing Captain Gosnold and the people in the bark. This speech was probably his address of welcome to the strangers, though of course it was wholly unintelligible to all except the savages themselves. When the speech was finished the boat advanced and came alongside the bark, and all the savages climbed up boldly on board.

The commander of the party was dressed in various garments which were evidently of European origin. He wore a black worked vest, cloth trousers, cloth stockings, shoes, and a hat, with a black band around it, such as denotes mourning, all in European style. The rest of the company—there were eight in all—were dressed in the Indian costume, which consisted of a simple garment about the loins, and a sort of shawl or blanket made of skins, over their shoulders. Their eyebrows were painted white, and they were armed with bows and arrows.

The company on board the ship endeavored to communicate with the savages, but as they were almost entirely dependent upon the language of signs, it was very little that either party could make the other understand. Captain Gosnold tried to ask his visitors where and how they obtained their boat, and the various other European articles which were in their possession, but he did not succeed very well in gaining any satisfactory information. Some of the English people thought that the savages meant to say by their signs that they obtained them from a Portuguese vessel that had come upon that coast a fishing, some time before.

The savages knew some English words, however, and named certain places on the coast which were known to Captain Gosnold. The chief of them also drew, with a piece of chalk, a sort of map of the coast in that vicinity, representing upon it the general course of the shore, and the principal islands, bays, and headlands.

In a word, the savages seemed to be very much pleased at the arrival of the strangers on their coast, and not only gave them a cordial welcome, but conducted themselves in all respects in a very obliging and friendly manner.

FARTHER PROGRESS WESTWARD

They expressed, too, by signs, their desire that Captain Gosnold would remain with them some time, and go and visit them on shore. But Captain Gosnold decided that it would not be best for him to do this. There was no safe anchorage there for his vessel, the whole coast being open and exposed. Besides a storm seemed then to be actually gathering, so he concluded that he must leave the coast again, and pursue his course toward the southward and westward, after first going out far enough to sea to be safe from the rocks and shoals that lined the shore.

So he dismissed his savage visitors and made sail, and was soon out of sight of land again.

It was three o'clock in the afternoon when the bark sailed away from the coast; the visit from the Indians having occupied all the forenoon. That evening and night the wind was high, and the sea was heavy. The bark made a good deal of progress southward, however, and the next day, as the weather moderated, they stood in again for land. They now found some islands between which and the mainland there was sheltered water. They came to anchor here, and then Captain Gosnold, taking with him four men, in one of the boats, went to the shore.

Passage to the Shore

The party going in the boat provided themselves with a good supply of fishing tackle, in hopes to take some fish, either going or returning, and also armed themselves with muskets to defend themselves from the Indians on the land, if there should be any occasion.

It was a charming day, though warm, and the people in the boat found the water everywhere alive with fish, which were swimming in shoals, in all directions. There were mackerel, herring, and other small fish in great abundance, and when they put their lines down, they brought up cod from a depth of about seven fathoms of water, as fast as they could pull them in. This was the more surprising to them, from the fact that off the coast of Newfoundland, which was at that time the great region of the cod fishery, the fish were only found at a depth of forty or fifty fathoms.

At length the boat reached the land, and was at once drawn up on a beautiful beach of white sand, which here lined the shore. Captain Gosnold left a guard to take care of the boat, and then he and the rest of the party took the muskets, and set off over the sand hills, full of interest and curiosity, on an excursion into the interior.

The Reconnaissance

The object of Captain Gosnold in this excursion into the interior was to gain some elevation from which he could make a reconnaissance, or survey, of the surrounding country. He wished to ascertain whether the land before him was an island or a portion of the main; and also what was the course and conformation of the coast in each direction. So he went on, followed by his attendants and companions, looking out for the highest land that they could see. The day was pleasant, but the sun was hot, and the ways which they had to traverse were difficult and sandy; so that, loaded as they were with the heavy muskets which they had to carry, the men became very weary before their march was ended.

They, however, went on perseveringly, ascending all the hills they could see from which there was any hope of an extended view.

They found that the place which they were exploring was a narrow tongue of land, not many miles wide, and connected apparently with the main toward the west, while it extended toward the east farther than they could see. Captain Gosnold took careful surveys of the surrounding country from several different elevations, and then, when the afternoon was so far spent that he could not safely be absent longer from his vessel, he set out on his return. As the party were returning toward their boat, there suddenly appeared a young Indian, coming out of the bushes. He was armed with a bow and arrows, and he had copper ornaments hanging in his ears. He did not seem at all afraid of the strangers, but, on the contrary, showed a very friendly disposition toward them, and tried to assist them by every means in his power. He kept with them until they reached the boat, and there, when they embarked, took leave of them on the shore.

The Name Cape Cod

The party returned to the ship, finding the fish as abundant in the water on the way, as they had done in the morning. They caught a great quantity of cod—so many, in fact, that when they got back to the vessel they had more than they knew what to do with, and were obliged to throw great numbers away. On account of the abundance of this species of fish in these waters, Captain Gosnold named the long tongue of land which he had been exploring, Cape Cod, which name it ever after retained.

Cruising among the Islands

Leaving the coast again, Captain Gosnold went on, until at length he fell in with the group of islands which lie off the southern coast of Massachusetts, and near the entrance to Buzzard's Bay. We have not space to describe in detail the movements of the expedition among these islands, the different landings which the party made, and the interviews with the Indians which took place, and other things that occurred. Captain Gosnold gave names to the different islands and points of land which he observed and visited, and though the name of Cape Cod remains to this day, as he appropriated it, some other designations which he proposed became subsequently displaced. He touched at a small island which he called Martha's Vineyard, on account of the great number of vines which he found growing there. But the name Martha's Vineyard was afterwards, in some way, transferred to a much larger island lying to the northward, and the original Martha's Vineyard is now known by the name of No Man's Land.

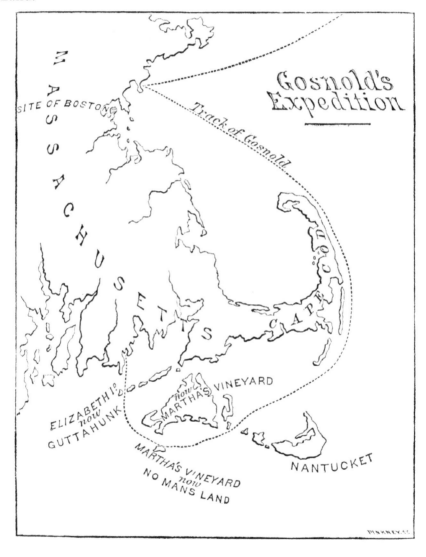

Gosnold also discovered the famous cliff, formed of many colored strata of sand and clay, which is now called Gay Head. Gosnold named it Dover Cliff. He passed round this cliff and came finally to anchor, near an island—the last of a group or range of islands, extending in a line towards a projecting point of the mainland—which he called Elizabeth Island. The whole range are now called Elizabeth Islands, and the one to which Gosnold first gave this name, is now known by its old Indian name of Cuttahunk.

As soon as the vessel was properly secured, the party began to make arrangements for exploring the neighboring shores by means of their boats.

APPEARANCE OF THE COUNTRY

Wherever the English landed, they were charmed with the fertility and beauty of the country, which, at this season of the year, was clothed in its richest attire. They found a great abundance of plants growing, which attracted their attention, such as peas, strawberries, whortleberries, raspberries, and also trees of many kinds that would be useful for building and other mechanical purposes. There were also great numbers of vines running up upon the trees, and growing so luxuriantly in some places, as almost entirely to envelop them, and conceal them from view. Of course, all these fruit bearing plants were only interesting as showing what the land would produce in the proper season, for it was too early yet for anything but blossoms to be borne upon them.

They also found plenty of excellent building stone, and pretty lakes of fresh water, and springs, and running streams, and groves of trees, and grass growing luxuriantly in natural meadows, and every other mark and token of a country extremely eligible for the habitation of man.

In order to try the fertility of the soil, they prepared a small plot of ground, and planted peas and beans in it, and, in a fortnight, the plants had grown up a foot in height.

They met parties of Indians from time to time, and held very friendly intercourse with them. Sometimes these interviews took place on the land, and sometimes the Indians came off in their canoes to the vessel. Sometimes when the party from the bark were sailing along the shore, a troop of Indians would follow them for a considerable distance, running along the beach, making signs of friendship, and uttering exclamations of delight at so strange a spectacle.

PLAN OF THE PROPOSED SETTLEMENT

After spending many days in cruising about among these islands, and exploring thoroughly all the sounds, and bays, and inlets, which they found, and often going on shore to make excursions and observations on the land, finally, about the end of May, the party made selection of a spot for the commencement of a settlement.

Their plan was to erect two buildings very near together, a dwelling and a fort—the one to furnish them, so far as practicable, with the comforts and conveniences of a habitation in peaceful and prosperous times, and the other a place of refuge and defense in case of war.

These two buildings together were to be large enough to accommodate the whole number that was to be left behind, when the bark returned to England. The men thus left were to employ themselves during the summer in making farms in the vicinity of their fort, and cultivating the land. In the autumn Gosnold was to return and bring them reinforcements, and fresh supplies.

In the meantime, during Gosnold's absence, the little colony, besides attending to their farming, were to cultivate a good understanding with the Indians, and to trade with them for such articles as they might have to sell, which consisted chiefly of skins and furs, and particularly of the bark and roots of an aromatic tree called sassafras, which grew abundantly in all that region, and was greatly prized in Europe in those days on account of its medicinal properties.

As they knew very well, however, that they could not certainly rely on maintaining a good understanding with the Indians, it was necessary to make their house a fortress, and to choose such a situation for it as should make it as secure as possible against any attack, and especially against a surprise.

Site Selected

After carefully exploring the whole region, Captain Gosnold at length made choice of an island which he called Elizabeth Island, in honor of Queen Elizabeth, who was then reigning in England. The whole group to which this island belongs are called the Elizabeth Islands to this day.

The chief reason which decided Gosnold and his party to make choice of this island for the first station of the proposed colony, was, that there was upon it a fresh water lake, of about two miles in circuit, that is, about three quarters of a mile across, and in this lake was a small islet, with a rocky margin, and containing about an acre of ground. They determined to build their fort upon this islet. The islet itself was in some sense a natural stronghold, its situation being such as to give its occupants a great advantage in resisting an attack from any species of force assailing them. And what was, perhaps, a still more important advantage, considering the wily and treacherous character of the Indians, it afforded excellent means for guarding against anything like surprise. The sentinels on the walls of their fort, or from the loopholes in it, could survey the waters of the lake at all times, on every side, so that it would be impossible for an enemy to approach without giving the garrison warning.

The little islet was covered with trees and underbrush, and the shores of it, as well as the shores of the lake all around, together with all the bays and indentations formed in them, were filled with vast flocks of wild fowl of different kinds, that fed among the sedges in the water, and built their nests in the margin of the forest which bordered the lake on every side.

The Work Commenced

The whole party immediately commenced the preliminary operations on the islet. Some were set at work to clear the ground of the trees and underbrush which encumbered it, reserving from the stems of the trees all such as were suitable for their building, and burning everything else. Another party commenced building a flat-bottomed boat, to serve as a means of transportation, to and from the islet; the shallop, or the ship's boat, being kept outside, of course, for communication between the ship and the shore. In two or three days these preparatory works were in a great measure accomplished, so that on the first of June the men began upon the fort itself.

The principal point was at first to get a portion of the structure sufficiently enclosed by walls and roof to keep out the weather, so that the supplies of provisions from the vessel which were to be left for the sustenance of the colony, while the bark returned to England, might be brought on shore from the vessel, and put in store there. For several days this work was pushed on very diligently. Cellars were dug under the buildings for the safekeeping of such articles, through the winter, as would be injured by frost. These cellars were walled up with stone. The buildings erected over them were formed of logs, the interstices between the logs in the wall being plastered with clay. The logs forming the roof, which were smaller and lighter than the others, were to be covered with a thatch of furze. The whole plot of ground was to be enclosed also with a stout and high palisade, as a protection against the Indians.

The men that were expected to remain and occupy the buildings were the ones chiefly employed in constructing them. The others, those who were to go back to England were engaged, while the work of building was going on, in making excursions with Captain Gosnold, in the surrounding region, or in digging sassafras to be put on board the vessel for a return cargo.

EXCURSIONS OF CAPTAIN GOSNOLD

In one of these excursions Captain Gosnold passed over to the mainland, and visited the shore there, near where the town of New Bedford now stands. He often met the Indians on such excursions, and they generally appeared very friendly. He and his men complained, however, that the Indians were very thievish, and they relate several instances of their stealing such articles as they took a fancy to, and seem to regard these depredations as proofs of great depravity on their part.

And yet they very quietly relate that at one time Captain Gosnold, in cruising about the shores with some of his men, came suddenly upon a party of four Indians, who were there with their canoe; the Indians being frightened, ran off into the woods, and then Captain Gosnold took their canoe, and brought it away with him to his ship, and there kept it, to take home to England as a curiosity!

It seems to have been by such conduct as this on the part of Europeans, that the friendly feelings which the aborigines of this country at first felt for the white men, were changed, in process of time, into deadly hatred, and insatiable thirst for revenge.

CURIOSITY OF THE INDIANS

At the various interviews which took place between the Indians and Captain Gosnold's men, a great deal of interest and curiosity was excited on each side, by the articles of food and of dress, and the various instruments and utensils, possessed and employed by the other. The Indians were particularly eager to touch, and handle, and taste everything. Some knives which were given to a chieftain on one occasion, being very bright and sharp, seemed to excite his wonder in the highest degree. "He beheld them," says the narrator of this account, "with great marvell." At another time when some Indians came out to the ship, "they stayed to take dinner on board, and did eat of our baccaleure" (whatever that may be), "and mustard, and drank of our beer. But the mustard nipping them in their noses, they could not endure. It was a sport to behold their faces made being bitten therewith."

AN ALARM FOR THE BUILDING PARTY

During the absence of Captain Gosnold on one of his excursions, the party at work upon the fort were thrown into a state of great alarm, and for a time they seemed to be in serious difficulty and danger.

In most cases, Captain Gosnold took the shallop when he went on these expeditions, leaving the bark at her anchorage off the shore, which thus furnished the men on the land a sure refuge and retreat, in case of accident or danger. In this instance, however, he took the vessel itself, leaving the men engaged on the islet, ten in all, to spend the night in the unfinished building. He promised to return the next day, and left the men accordingly only sufficient provisions for three meals.

But the next day the captain did not come, and in the afternoon, the men, who had now consumed all the food left for them, began to feel very anxious. They did not know what the cause of the detention might be, nor how long it might continue. Even if no serious accident had happened, there was danger, in case the wind should get into the southwest, that the bark might not be able to return for some days.

THE SEARCH FOR FOOD

The officer in command of the fort concluded to send out a detachment of his men in search of food. He thought that they would be able to procure some crabs, or lobsters, or turtles, among the creeks and inlets of the island, which would, at least, suffice to keep the party from starving. He accordingly despatched a company of four on this expedition. After going off to some distance, and not being very successful in their hunting, the men divided themselves into two parties of two each, to go in different directions, in hopes of thus increasing their chance of finding food. After a long and fruitless ramble, in the course of which they became entangled in the swamps, and lost their way, one of the parties returned to the fort. The other, when night was coming on, fell unexpectedly upon a camp of Indians. The Indians at once attacked them with arrows, and wounded one of the men in the side. "The other," as the account states, "a lusty, and nimble fellow, leaped in and cut their bow strings, whereupon they fled."

It was, by this time, getting quite dark, and the two men were entirely unable to find their way. So they spent the night in the woods. Their friends at the fort were, of course, extremely anxious on their account. They were, besides, wholly destitute of proper food, and were obliged to make their supper, as they best could, out of greens, and roots, and nuts, which they gathered from the ground around them.

The next day, however, the two lost men returned, and soon after they came in the whole company heard the sound of the captain's voice, hailing them from the shore. The bark had returned. The sound of the captain's voice, they said, in the account which they gave of these transactions, "made such music as sweeter never came unto poor men."

DIFFICULTIES

The blockhouse, or fort, which had been commenced on the islet, by Gosnold's party, is supposed to have been the first building, intended to be a permanent structure, that was undertaken by Europeans, on any portion of the northern coasts of America; and if the colony had succeeded in establishing itself, and permanently maintaining its ground, the little islet on which the fort was built, and the lake, or pond, whose waters protected the shores of it, would have been as celebrated in American history, as Plymouth afterward became. But the plan, unfortunately, was not destined to succeed. Difficulties and dissensions of various kinds had been already gradually creeping in among the different parties composing the expedition. Some of those who had intended to remain in the country, when the bark returned, found their hearts failing them as the time drew near. The idea of being left alone in the midst of those vast solitudes, with nothing but wildernesses and wastes of water all around them, and forests occupied only by wild beasts and prowling savages, awakened in their minds, as the time drew near, feelings of solemn awe, which gradually ripened into fear. Some began to apprehend that Captain Gosnold, if he once returned to Europe with the bark, would not come back again, and that those who should remain behind would be left to perish of starvation.

Besides these suspicions and fears, disagreements and quarrels broke out among the men, owing partly to inevitable differences of opinion in regard to the course which was to be pursued, and partly to the evil influence of certain unreasonable and unmanageable members of the company. In a word, long before the buildings were so far completed as to become habitable, the company became greatly demoralized.

Abandonment of the Enterprise

In consequence of these things a feeling of discouragement spread rapidly among the people. One after another of the number began to express some doubt whether he should remain, or return in the vessel. And when finally a division came to be made of the food, and it was found how small a portion there was to be left with the colony—amounting, as they calculated, to only a six weeks' supply, when it would be at least six *months* before they could expect the bark to come back—they one and all concluded to abandon their fort, and return to England together.

This decision was arrived at near the middle of June, just about a fortnight after they commenced the work of building their fort and dwelling.

Preparations for the Return to England

Nothing was now to be done but to fill up the bark as soon as possible with such commodities as could be obtained, that would be of value in England. These commodities were sassafras, cedar wood, furs, skins, and the like. The men worked diligently a week longer in making up the cargo, and then set sail for England. They touched at Gay Head and No Man's Land, or as they called them, Dover Cliff and Martha's Vineyard, on their way, and there procured fresh supplies of fish and fowls, and then turned their course out over the broad Atlantic.

They returned much quicker than they came. Sailors say it is downhill from America to England, and uphill from England to America. The truth is, that the prevailing winds and currents on the North Atlantic are from west to east; and this renders it much easier to make progress in one direction than in the other, especially for vessels that are dependent upon sails. Thus, although the bark was about fifty-seven days in coming from Falmouth to No Man's Land, they returned from No Man's Land to Falmouth in thirty-five, having been absent from England four months almost to a day.

This voyage of Gosnold's may be considered as a specimen of the numerous expeditions which were fitted out in those days to the coasts of America—displaying great energy, valor and fortitude on the part of those who embarked in them, but based all on delusive ideas and expectations, and leading to no result.

Beginning of Difficulty with the Indians

One thing is quite remarkable in the accounts of these expeditions which have come down to us, and that is the frequent disregard of all the principles of justice and good faith in the manner in which these parties of adventurers treated the natives of the country. They continually, in their narratives, denounced the thievishness and treachery of the Indians, and then coolly relate acts of robbery and faithlessness on their own part as if the obligations of honesty and truth were all on one side, and pagans and savages had no rights which Christians were bound to respect. They would entice the Indians on board their ships, and then keep them as prisoners. In repeated instances they took them to England for the purpose of showing them as curiosities, and also to teach them English so that they might come back with them, on subsequent voyages, and serve as interpreters. In one instance, at least, the commander of a vessel seized and secured twenty Indians, whom he contrived to inveigle on board his ship, and carried them off to the Island of Malaga and sold them as slaves, for a sum equal to a hundred dollars a-piece—"which," says the narrator of the account, "raises such an enmity in the savages against our nation, as makes further attempts at commerce with them very dangerous."

The dealings of the Indians with the white men seem, on the other hand, in many instances at least, to have been just and humane. Cases occurred of persons who had been wrecked on the coast, from vessels that came to fish, and so had fallen into the hands of the natives, and had subsequently been preserved and protected by them, and afterward ransomed by their countrymen in subsequent voyages. In some cases, however, it would seem that they treated such captives with great cruelty.

SOME ADVANTAGE GAINED

Thus the coasts of the northern part of America were visited by a great number of vessels, at one time and another, during the early part of the seventeenth century, and though no permanent settlement was yet made, a great deal was learned in respect to the character of the country, the conformation of the coast, the nature of the climate, the soil and the productions, and the habits and dispositions of the savages. Thus the way was prepared for the Pilgrim Fathers of New England to think of this country, among others, as their future abode when they found that they could no longer bear the hardships and oppressions to which they were subjected in their own native land.

CHAPTER II
THE PURITANS

The Name Virginia

During all the period referred to in the last chapter, when so many trading and exploring expeditions were sent out to America, the country which lay along the whole coast, now belonging to the United States, was called Virginia. The country was so named by those who first discovered it, in honor of Queen Elizabeth, who was, at that time, the reigning sovereign of England, and who, as she was never married, was often called the virgin queen. The southern portion of the region, was called South Virginia, and the northern, including what is now New York and New England, was North Virginia.

Thus Gosnold's expedition, though the island where he attempted to found his settlement, was in what is now Massachusetts, was considered then as an expedition to form a colony in North Virginia.

Ownership of the Territory

There is another thing which it is necessary to explain before proceeding with the story, and, that is, that the country extending along the whole line of this coast, and back to an indefinite distance into the interior, was considered as belonging to the British crown, on account of its having been discovered, and explored, by British navigators. Queen Elizabeth died, and was succeeded by King James I, before anything effectual was done toward making settlements in the country. King James, therefore, considered the territory as belonging to him, and no person could settle upon it, or even visit it, for the purpose of trading with the natives, without authority from him; and then, only on such terms and conditions as he should impose. As to any rights which the natives of the country might have to lands, which they and their ancestors had possessed in peace, from time immemorial, no one seemed to pay any regard to them. They seem to have been considered as only the pretended and imaginary rights of pagans and savages, with which Christian nations had no concern, except to make provision for the payment, from time to time, of moderate sums of money, to extinguish the claim of occupancy.

PLANS OF THE GOVERNMENT

After a time, in order to provide for the settlement of the country in a regular methodical manner, and to secure to the king his share of the gold and silver which might be found, and of the profits which might be made by traffic with the natives, the government determined to organize two companies of English merchants, to conduct the business of colonization on certain terms and conditions which they were to make with the king.

One of these companies was formed of merchants and other men of business, residing in London. This was called the London Company. The London Company received authority to make settlements in South Virginia.

The other company was formed of merchants and others—all men of wealth, standing, and influence—that lived in Plymouth, Exeter, and other towns, in that region, that is, in the southwestern part of England. This company was called the Plymouth Company, and they were authorized to send expeditions, and to establish colonies in North Virginia.

These two companies were established by the king in 1606. The limits of the territories assigned to them respectively, were not precisely defined, but to avoid disputes and quarrels, neither company was to attempt to establish any settlement within a hundred miles of any settlement of the other.

In following the history of these times, the reader must be careful not to confound the Plymouth *Company* with the Plymouth *colony,* a mistake which is very often made. The Plymouth *Company* was an association of rich, influential, and powerful men, living in England, in the town of Plymouth, and in other commercial towns around it. They had a charter from the king authorizing them to send expeditions to America, and to found colonies there, on paying to the king a certain portion of the profits they might realize. They subscribed money in shares, to buy vessels and to purchase stores. They had a complete organization in England—with their board of directors, and their rules and regulations, and their accountants, and offices for the transaction of business.

The Plymouth *colony,* on the other hand, was a company drawn from comparatively very humble stations in life, who made an arrangement with this rich and powerful company, to settle upon a portion of their land in America. They named the place of their settlement New Plymouth, in honor of Old Plymouth, in England, which was the seat of the great corporation above referred to.

Thus the Plymouth Company in England, and the Plymouth colony in America, were bodies of men as different from each other as can well be conceived. It was not even on account of the Plymouth Company, that the colony gave the name of Plymouth to their first settlement, but simply, because the port of Plymouth was the last at which they touched on leaving England, and consequently, it was at that point that they bade farewell, forever, to their native land. It happened, indeed, as will hereafter appear, that all the dealings of the Plymouth colonists, preliminary to their departure from England, were with the London Company, and not with the Plymouth Company, for it was in South Virginia, as it was called, that they intended to settle, when they formed their plans.

Various Undertakings of the Two Companies

As soon as the London and Plymouth companies were organized, they at once commenced fitting out expeditions to America, some for the purpose of fishing and trading on the coast, and others for attempting to establish settlements and colonies, as related in the last chapter. Of all these expeditions, the one that first succeeded in retaining their hold upon the coast, was the party that named their town Plymouth. This colony, therefore, being the first that succeeded, became subsequently the most famous, and the expedition by which it was established has become more celebrated than any other undertaking of the kind in the whole history of emigration to

America. The expedition was that of the Pilgrim Fathers, as they are called, who came over in the *Mayflower*.

IN WHAT SENSE PILGRIMS

They are called Pilgrims, because it was in a certain sense a religious impulse which induced them to make the voyage. It is only, however, in a figurative sense, that this word can be applied to them. Strictly speaking, pilgrims are those who make a journey or a voyage to visit some sacred shrine, with a view of paying their devotions there. But these men left all that was sacred and holy in their eyes, so far as religious thoughts and associations were concerned, and came to an utter wilderness, inhabited only by savages and pagans. Instead of journeying as real pilgrims do, from a less to a more sacred place, in order to draw from it, as from a fountain, some new and fresh religious inspiration for themselves—they came away entirely beyond the pale both of religion and civilization, into a region where their piety, instead of receiving a fresh radiance from the halo of a sacred shrine, was to diffuse its own proper light, in illuminating one of the darkest regions of paganism.

Still, as they acted under the influence of religious feeling, and for the accomplishment of religious ends, in undertaking the enterprise, they have received the name in history, of the Pilgrim Fathers of New England.

CORRELATION OF POLITICS AND RELIGION IN RESPECT TO LIBERTY

The great Reformation in England, by which the English nation had separated itself from the Catholic Church, had taken place some years before this time, but it left the people very much divided in opinion, in respect to how far ceremonial observances should be retained in the church. It is a noticeable fact, and one almost universal, that aristocratic and monarchical ideas in government, and strong attachment to rites and ceremonies in religion, almost always go together. The reason seems to be this, that the greater the importance that is attached to rites and ceremonies is, the greater becomes the influence of the priests, or ministerial functionaries, by whom the rites and ceremonies are performed. Now a powerful clerical order in any state, if it can be kept under subjection to the political sovereignty, may be made a very efficient auxiliary, in carrying out government plans.

Despotic governments, therefore, almost always favor such views of religion as will most consolidate and increase the power of its ministers, as an ecclesiastical organization. Anything that tends to weaken the tie which binds the church together as a power, and to make religion a mere personal concern of individual men, they always oppose.

And even in governments more or less free, the differences which exist among different classes of people follow generally the same principle. This is by no means an universal rule—but it is a very general one. Those classes of the community that are more aristocratically inclined—and who are suspicious of the people, and think that there is no safety but in a strong government possessed of power to keep them under control, are more inclined to magnify clerical influence, and to favor those religious establishments in which the clerical organization and power is, nominally at least, most complete, and where the greatest significance and value are accorded to rites and forms. Whereas, on the other hand, so far as republican or democratic sentiments prevail, there is a tendency among those who embrace them, to be extremely jealous of everything like clerical power, to divest public worship, as far as may be, of outward form, and to make religion, as much as possible, a matter of private opinion, and feeling, to be governed by the reason and conscience of the individual man, under responsibility only to his Maker.

There is abundant room for being in the right or in the wrong, under either of these classes of opinion. There is, perhaps, quite as much danger of error in belief, or delusions in feeling, among the votaries of a purely spiritual faith, as there is of formality and hypocrisy in those who attach greater importance to forms, and to well organized clerical organizations. I do not mean, therefore, by what I have said, to condemn absolutely the one class and uphold the other, but only to state a fact which cannot be called in question, and the understanding of which is very necessary to a right comprehension of the difficulty which arose in England between King James and the Puritans.

THE PURITANS

The name Puritans was given to the class of persons in England who were in favor of what they called a purely spiritual religion, and opposed to everything like clerical influence and power, and to almost all forms, rites, and ceremonies, in public worship. The Puritans were, so to speak, the advanced guard of the Reformation, carrying their principles of hostility to popery to such a length that they could not endure a hierarchy in any form in church government, nor a liturgy of any kind in religious worship. Religion was with them a purely personal concern between man and God. They would take the Word of God, as they themselves individually understood it, as their rule of faith and practice, but refused to submit to any other spiritual authority. They claimed the right to form their own churches, choose their own ministers, and to act in all things pertaining to religion, in a manner wholly independent of the state, and of all other earthly authority.

IDEAS OF KING JAMES

These claims and pretensions did not comport with the ideas and plans of King James at all. James was king of Scotland when Elizabeth died, and as he was then the next heir to the throne of England he at once became sovereign of both realms. He had been well acquainted with the ideas of the Puritans in Scotland, and he saw at once how much the general prevalence of such ideas in his kingdom of England would curtail his own power. Accordingly, as he crossed the border and advanced into England to take possession of his new realm, he came determined to put down Puritanism and dissent by the most vigorous and decisive measures.

Nor are we to suppose because we differ from King James in opinion on these subjects, that acting as he did, he was guilty of doing what he knew was wrong, and of knowingly violating the most sacred rights of his subjects, from a selfish desire to lay broader foundations for his own greatness and power. He conceived of a kingdom as one great family, which ought to be bound together in one harmonious system of government, that should include and cover everything on which the welfare of the state depended, whether temporal or spiritual. He announced in the most public manner, on his accession to the throne, in answer to a petition asking that he would accord to his subjects the liberty of worship, according to their consciences, that "he would have none of that liberty as to ceremonies." He would have "one doctrine and one discipline—one religion, in substance and ceremony, throughout his kingdom." Presbyterianism, which was the form that Puritanism had assumed in Scotland, and the one in which he had chiefly seen its spirit and tendencies, "as well agrees with monarchy," he said, "as God with the devil." And he declared that he would make his people conform to the established religion of the country, or else "he would harry them out of the land—or do worse still by them."

The Conflict

Then followed a long conflict, which continued for many years, during which time the king and his government employed very severe measures to compel all the people, and especially all the ministers of the land, to conform to the rules and discipline of the established Church of England; but the heavier the pressure that was put upon the dissentients, the more disobedient and obstinate, as the king termed it, they became. It would require many volumes to describe the forms which this conflict assumed at different times, and in different parts of the kingdom, and to narrate the various incidents which grew out of it, and the particular cases of persecution and suffering which, from time to time, occurred to excite the special attention and sympathy of the community. The only result was to make each side more determined to persist than before, and to carry each one farther and farther toward the extreme.

One very curious phase of the controversy was that which related to the observance of Sunday. The king, in his desire to make as much as possible of the prescribed ceremonials of public worship, as performed by the clergy, desired to encourage the people in spending the rest of the day, after divine service was ended, in any manner which might be agreeable to them. The Puritans, on the other hand, maintained that religion being a spiritual service, the public worship of a congregation in a church was of secondary importance—that the whole of Sunday was to be set apart for the service of God, and the hours that were not spent in public prayer and praise should be devoted to private communion with God—which was, after all, the highest and most essential form of religious devotion. At length the king issued his proclamation, ordaining, "that those who attend church on Sundays should not be disturbed or discouraged from dancing, archery, leaping, vaulting, having May-games, whitson-ales, morrice-dances, setting up May-poles, and other sports therewith used, or any other such harmless recreation, on Sundays, after divine service." He required all the ministers in a certain portion of the realm, where Puritanism most prevailed, to read this proclamation from their pulpits, and those who refused to do it were summoned into court, and suspended from office.

The effect of this controversy was to fix the Puritans more firmly than ever in their determination to insist upon a strict observance of the Lord's day.

SCROOBY

Among the various congregations of Puritans, there was one, in the North of England, which was under the pastoral charge of a learned and devout minister, named John Robinson. There has been some uncertainty, in regard to the precise locality of this church, but it is now supposed to have been a small town on the northern borders of Nottinghamshire—and near the confines of Yorkshire, and Lincolnshire—named Scrooby. The principal person in the congregation was a gentleman of property and standing, named William Brewster.

It was at his house, in fact, that the congregation, which was drawn chiefly from the ranks of the common people, in and around Scrooby, were accustomed to assemble for religious worship; for the men who formed this congregation were so much in earnest in their opposition to what they considered the empty rites and ceremonies, and the lifeless formality of the church establishment, that they had entirely withdrawn from it, and had set up a church and a worship of their own.

THE SEPARATISTS

Many who were Puritans in sentiment and feeling, in various parts of England, had not proceeded to this extreme, but still retained a nominal connection with the established church, hoping to reform it. Those who withdrew entirely, as the Scrooby people had done, were called Separatists, and they, of course, brought upon themselves a double share of the animosity and hatred of the king.

PERSECUTION

It was not long before the king's government began to resort to the most decisive measures against all the Separatists, as they called them, in the realm. The Puritans who remained nominally connected with the establishment, could scarcely be tolerated in their covert and repressed disaffection, but those who withdrew and attempted to set up a worship of their own, were considered as in a state of actual rebellion. Some were arrested and imprisoned. Others were reprimanded, threatened, and fined. A watch was set over others in their houses, and their meetings for worship on Sundays were prohibited. If the congregations attempted to hold such meetings, the assemblies were broken up by the officers of the law. The Scrooby congregation were compelled to meet as they could, from house to house, in secrecy, and the members composing it were so pursued and harassed in their private avocations, that life became a burden to them. At last they began to consider the question of abandoning their native land altogether, and seeking the liberty of worshiping God according to their own conscience, in some foreign land. The only land which seemed open to them, as a place of refuge, was Holland.

DIFFICULTIES AND DISCOURAGEMENTS

Holland was a republic, and as might have been expected, a far greater degree of religious liberty was allowed there by the government, than in any other country in Europe. Still the difficulties in the way of the Puritans, in attempting to emigrate thither, were almost overwhelming. In the first place, it was not probable that the government would allow them to go, unless they could contrive to go by stealth. Then they were not rich, and the little property which they could command, it would be very difficult for them to remove. On their arrival in Holland, also, they would have the language to learn, and new modes of earning their livelihood to acquire, and many other trial and troubles to meet, incident always to the situation of strangers in a foreign land. Still, after mature deliberation, and finding the pressure of persecution growing harder and heavier upon them every day, they determined to make the attempt. But the hardships and sufferings which they were compelled to endure in their endeavor to escape from the country, far exceeded their worst anticipations.

THE TROUBLE AT BOSTON

One of the nearest and most convenient ports for them to embark at, was that of Boston, which lies on the eastern coast of England, nearly opposite to Scrooby.[1] They determined to provide the means of embarking a portion of the company at this place, and as they found, on enquiry, that the government would not allow them to go away openly, they were obliged to procure a vessel wholly for their use, and to pay an extraordinary price for it, and to give fees to the sailors, in order to induce them to assist the party in getting away privately. A place was appointed on the coast, near Boston, where they were all to be in readiness, with such furniture and goods as they were to carry with them, and the vessel was to come for them there, and take them all on board in the night.

The men with their families accordingly went to the place of rendezvous, at the appointed time, but the vessel was not there. They

---

[1] See map on page 47.

waited long in vain. At length the vessel came, and they were taken on board, but they found immediately afterward that they had been betrayed—for no sooner were they embarked, than a company of soldiers came out to the vessel and made them prisoners. They were all brought on shore again in open boats, being searched, and rifled of all their money and valuables on the way.

As soon as they were landed they were taken into the public square in the town, and there exhibited to the people, who came flocking around them to mock and deride them. After a time they were conducted to prison, and word was sent to the king, stating that they had been captured in the attempt to escape from the country, and asking what was to be done with them.

The end of it was, that after being kept in prison for a month, the greater portion of them were set at liberty, and sent back to their former homes, destitute and wretched.

BRADFORD AND HIS BOOKS

Among the company, on this occasion, was a very talented and accomplished young man, named Bradford, who afterward became greatly distinguished in the history of the Plymouth colony, as its governor. When he was only twelve years old he was observed as a sedate youth, of grave countenance and earnest manner, who was a constant attendant at the meetings. He was only about eighteen years of age, when he joined the church at Scrooby, and he evinced a great deal of independence and resolution in taking this step, as he was directly opposed in it by a large circle of influential friends. He was still very young at the time of the attempted emigration, and though he held no office in the church, he was greatly esteemed by all the members of it, on account of his business talents, and the great efficiency and energy of his character. He had a library of about three hundred volumes with him, among the goods that he attempted to take away. These books were seized in one of the boats, but were afterwards given up, and Bradford himself was released on account of his youth. His books he took afterward with him to America, and there remains an inventory and appraisal of them, made at his death. The appraisal was "forty-three pounds in silver money."

THE EMBARKATION AT HULL

The company did not despair on account of the failure at Boston. The same persons, joined by some others, the next spring made another attempt. They found a vessel that belonged in Holland, in the port of Hull, which is another town on the eastern shore of England. They explained the circumstances of their case to the captain of this vessel, and proposed to him to take them over with him, on his return to his own country. He said he would do so, and bid them not fear. He was sure, he said, that he could manage the business safely.

A rendezvous was appointed in a solitary place on the coast, at some distance from Hull, where it was supposed that the embarkation could be safely effected. The women and children were to be taken to the place in a sailboat—following the line of the shore. The men, for whom there was not room enough in the sailboat, and who were able to walk, were to proceed to the place on foot. All were to be there at a certain appointed time.

DETENTION OF THE WOMEN AND CHILDREN

Thus far everything was encouraging. The vessel, and also the company of men, arrived at the proposed place of embarkation at the appointed time, but the sailboat had not come. On enquiring, it was found that the sailboat was aground in a small creek, where she had put in the night before. The reason for this was, that the sea was so rough, on account of a heavy swell which was rolling in from the offing, and the women and children suffered so much from seasickness, and became so wet and cold, that their condition became truly deplorable. While in this state, they came—in following the coast—to a small creek, or inlet, and it was concluded to go in and seek shelter for a time, until the sea should go down. But while in the creek the boat had got aground, and now the company on board were waiting for the tide to rise. It was early in the morning, and the tide would not be up to float the sailboat until about noon.

When these facts were ascertained, and reported to the captain of the vessel, he thought, that as there was no time to lose, it would be better for the men to be brought on board at once. The men he knew had arrived, for from the deck of his vessel, which lay a little way off the land, he could see them walking about upon the shore.

A Surprise

He accordingly sent the boat on shore to bring the men off to the vessel, so that they might be already embarked when the sailboat should come with the women and children. One boatload was brought, and the men put safely on board; but as the boat was returning for the rest, suddenly the captain of the vessel saw a squadron of horsemen coming at full speed toward the spot, across a plain which here bordered the shore. He knew at once that these must be the king's troops. He was greatly alarmed, and immediately recalled his boat, and made all sail, in order to escape from the coast, taking with him the boatload of men who were already on board.

Distress of the Men Embarked

These men were, of course, plunged into a state of the greatest terror and distress. Not only were their companions, that were left behind on the beach, certain to be overwhelmed and made prisoners by the horsemen, but what was infinitely worse, the sailboat containing their wives and children would undoubtedly be discovered and seized, and the helpless ones on board would be subject to the most cruel treatment. Even in case of their being released by the soldiers, their inevitable fate would be to wander as outcasts about the country, friendless and destitute, and with nothing but the charity of people that hated and despised them, to save them from perishing of hunger.

They were all perfectly unprovided for. They had not with them in the sailboat, even a change of clothes for themselves or their children—all their baggage, of every kind, having been previously put on board the vessel.

As might have been expected, the men on board the vessel were perfectly frantic at seeing the troop of horsemen come on to seize all that were dear to them, while they were borne helplessly away, without the possibility of doing anything to succor their loved ones,

Attempted embarkation for Holland.

or even to share their fate. They begged and entreated the captain to return and put them on shore. They would have given all they possessed could they have induced him to do so. But he was inflexible. He knew that he himself would be seized by the English soldiers, if he were to put himself in their power. So he crowded all sail, and steered directly out to sea, while his poor suffering passengers could only stand upon the deck, overwhelmed with distress and anguish, and watch the receding coast in despair, as it gradually disappeared from view.

A STORM

But this was not the end of their troubles. The storm, which had been gathering for some time, now came on with great fury. The vessel was driven far from her course, and came at length near being wrecked upon the coast of Norway. At one time she was thrown on her beam ends, and she shipped such heavy seas, that the mariners and the people on board were, for a time, up to their necks in water.

At length, however, the storm abated, and then the vessel, with infinite difficulty, was able to make its way to its destined port in Holland.

FATE OF THOSE LEFT BEHIND

In the meantime, some of the men who remained on the shore, when they saw the troop coming, were alert enough to elude them, and make their escape. The others chose to remain and share the fate of their wives and children, who, they knew, must certainly fall into the soldiers' hands. They thought that, by remaining, they might possibly be of some assistance to them. At any rate, they could not endure to leave them to suffer seizure and maltreatment alone. And when the soldiers found the sailboat, and took possession of it, "it was pitiful," as one of the sufferers said, in afterwards describing the scene, "to see the heavy case of these poor women in their distress—what weeping and crying on every side—some for their husbands that were carried away in the ship—others, not knowing what would become of them and their little ones. Others melted in tears, seeing their poor little ones hanging about them, crying for fear, and quaking with cold."

The soldiers took the whole company off, and delivered them over to the authorities. The authorities hurried them about from place to place, not knowing what to do with them. They could not well punish them by imprisoning them, for it was very clear that the blame—whatever there might be of blame in this attempted escape from the country—must fall upon the men, and not upon their wives and children, whose only fault was that of adhering to and following their husbands. They could not send them to their homes, for now they had no homes in England to go to—their houses and little farms, on which they lived, having been sold and disposed of in other ways. The government were, in a word, quite embarrassed to know what to do with their prisoners, now they had taken them, and so, after moving them from place to place for a while in their uncertainty, and harassing them in every possible way until they were at last reduced to the extreme of misery and distress—they finally let them go.

FINAL ESCAPE TO HOLLAND

The poor fugitives at last contrived to escape, in small parties, and in various ways, to Holland. Mr. Robinson, Mr. Brewster, and the other principal members of the congregation, remained in England till the last, doing all in their power to succor their suffering brethren, and to help them to make their escape. When at length all the rest had embarked, they followed, and in due time the whole company were once more collected together in the place which they intended to make their future home—which was the city of Amsterdam.

CHAPTER III
THE VOYAGE OF THE *MAYFLOWER*

Holland

Holland, though it seems a very remote, and an exceedingly foreign and outlandish country to us, was not so by any means, in those days, to the people living on the eastern shores of England. The distance across, over the German Ocean, was not more than one hundred and fifty miles, and there had been for a long time a great deal of commercial intercourse between the two countries, the English ports being visited every year by Dutch vessels, and the Dutch ports by English vessels in great numbers. English merchants too, often established branches of their houses in Holland, and this caused many English families to settle there—the families, namely, of the clerks, porters, mechanics, seamen, and other persons connected with the international commerce. Then besides this, on account of some political arrangements which had been made between the Dutch and English governments, several towns in Holland had been delivered up to English custody, and were garrisoned by English troops, and this greatly increased the intercommunication between the two countries. From these various causes, it resulted that the Puritan emigrants were not, after all, when they reached Amsterdam, so entirely in a land of strangers and foreigners, as we might, at first, without understanding the true state of the case, have been disposed to imagine.

Still, their condition was one of great hardship. Their property, which had never been great, was very much reduced by the sacrifices which they had been obliged to make in closing up their affairs in England, and by the expenses and the damages incurred in their removal. They had also the language of their new country to learn, and to find new ways and means of earning a livelihood.

DANGER OF BEING DRAWN INTO A QUARREL

There was another very serious difficulty which threatened the Robinson congregation in Amsterdam, very soon after their arrival, and that was the danger of being drawn into a church quarrel there. It seems that theirs was not the only congregation of Puritans which had come from England to seek refuge in Amsterdam. There were two others, and between these two, some sort of a difficulty had arisen which threatened to become a serious quarrel. Robinson found that there was danger that his people might be drawn into this dispute, and to avoid it, he and Brewster determined to remove to some other place.

REMOVAL TO LEYDEN

They finally made choice of Leyden, which was then, as it is now, a quiet and beautiful town, situated about twenty miles from Amsterdam, and more in the interior of the country. Robinson at once wrote to the magistrates at Leyden, asking permission for his congregation to come there and take up their abode. A favorable answer was received, and the whole company accordingly removed to Leyden. This was about the year 1609.

RESIDENCE IN LEYDEN

The colony, for the congregation may be now considered in the light of a colony, remained about eleven years in Leyden. Of course, they had at first many obstacles and difficulties to encounter, and many hardships to bear; but they were so patient under their trials, and so industrious and faithful in their several callings, that they soon made many friends, and their condition rapidly improved. They at once, as one of the number says, in his account of these transactions, "fell to such trades and employments as they could individually best succeed in—valuing peace and their spiritual comfort above any other riches whatever. At length they were able to make a comfortable living, though not without hard and continual labor. Enjoying much sweet and delightful society and spiritual comfort together, they grew in knowledge, and in other gifts and graces of the Spirit of God, and lived together in peace, and love, and holiness. And many came unto them from different parts of England, so as they grew to a great congregation."

BREWSTER

Brewster himself, who had been from the beginning the principal man in the congregation—the only one, in fact, who was possessed at the outset of any considerable property, suffered, it seems, for a while, even more than the rest. His property had all been taken from him, and his habits of life had been such as to unfit him for the laborious mechanical trades to which the others resorted. He was a gentleman and a scholar, but it was very difficult for him to make his talents and attainments serviceable in the way of earning a living. At length he succeeded in obtaining employment as a teacher of the English language. There was so much intercourse in those days between Holland and England, from causes which have already been explained, that many persons among the higher classes in Leyden, and in other Dutch cities, desired to learn the English language. Brewster was a good Latin scholar, and his knowledge of that language, which is in part the foundation of the English tongue, and his acquaintance with the philosophical principles of language in general, which a right study of the ancient languages is sure to impart, gave him great success as a teacher.

Beginning in this way, he gradually advanced until at length he obtained means to establish a printing office, and to print in it a number of English books, especially of such kinds as were not allowed to be printed in England. His doing this excited the ill will of the English ambassador at Leyden, who watched his proceedings very narrowly, and made unfavorable representations in respect to him to the government at home. But being within the jurisdiction of a foreign government, King James could not molest him. So he continued the work of printing and circulating useful publications for some time, quite successfully.

DANGER OF THE YOUNG MEN

Things went on in this way for some years, in the course of which time, the company of emigrants had gradually surmounted nearly all the difficulties and dangers which they had apprehended in removing to a foreign land, but then, at length, a new difficulty—one which apparently they had not much thought of, at first—began to appear and to assume alarming proportions. This new cause of anxiety and alarm arose from the danger which threatened the morals and the character of the young men. The boys and girls—who, when the colony left England, had been mere children, were now growing up to be young men and women, and their parents began to find that the circumstances under which they were placed, were exerting a very unfavorable influence upon them in respect to their moral and religious character. These young people, as they grew up, learned the language of the country, and with it they learned much that was evil. Many of them fell into bad company, and were in danger of being led away into vicious courses by the influence of dissolute companions. Others imbibed the martial spirit which then prevailed in Europe, and wished to enlist in the armies. Others still, who were saved from these dangers by the watchfulness and care of their parents, or by the gracious influences of the Spirit of God in their hearts, were so oppressed by the incessant confinement and toil, necessary to enable them to gain a livelihood in so densely populated a city, that their health was impaired, their growth impeded, and they became weak, decrepit, and infirm, at the time when they ought to be attaining to the strength and vigor of manhood.

These evils, which were at first not felt, or even perhaps anticipated, gradually increased, until at length, about eight or ten years after they settled at Leyden, the hearts of all the parents in the company were filled with distress and anxiety.

THE RESOLUTION TO REMOVE TO AMERICA

The result of the many and anxious consultations, which the leading members of the congregation held with each other and with their pastor on this subject, was the determination to close up their business and all their affairs in Leyden, and emigrate to some place in America, where they could live in a community by themselves—and also, as they fondly imagined, could, by beginning at the foundation, build up a social state on such moral and religious principles as should secure the temporal and spiritual welfare of themselves and their descendants forever.

They seem to have been fully aware of all the difficulties and dangers attending such an undertaking. The long and dangerous voyage—the hardships to which women and children, already enervated by the confinement and toil which they had been subjected to for so many years, would be exposed—the difficulties and the perils unavoidable in attempting to commence a settlement in an uncivilized and uncultivated country—the cruelty, treachery, and violence which they were to expect from the natives, in case of disagreement with them—these, and many other such considerations, were brought fully before their minds, and so serious and threatening did these dangers appear, that many of the congregation, especially those who were somewhat advanced in years, were appalled at the difficulties and hazards of the undertaking, and could not make up their minds to embark in it.

A certain portion, however, after carefully considering the subject in all its bearings, concluded that it was best for them to go. Of the rest, many intended to follow as soon as the establishment of the new colony should be successfully accomplished.

APPLICATION TO KING JAMES

One of the most important points to be secured at the outset, was some sort of agreement with the English government, authorizing them to settle in America, and stipulating that they should not be molested there in the free exercise of their religion; for the whole of the northern part of America was claimed to be within the jurisdiction of the king of England. So they sent two of their number to England to make application to the king. They drew up a statement of their opinions and principles in as conciliatory a form as possible, disavowing all want of loyalty to the government, and all desire to create any difficulty or dissension among his majesty's subjects; and they asked the king to give them authority to proceed to America, and settle there under his protection.

But the king would not give them any formal grant or authorization whatever. He said they might go if they chose, and as long as they behaved well it was probable that he should not molest them—but that he would not give them any written pledge, or do anything which would prevent his pursuing such a course with them, in time to come, as he should judge proper.

APPLICATION TO THE LONDON COMPANY

The same commissioners were to apply to the London Company, to whom, as has already been related, the king had granted the exclusive right to establish settlements in the southern part of the country. They applied to the London Company, and not to the Plymouth Company, because they had concluded, after a great deal of deliberation and inquiry, that it would be best, on the whole, for them to establish their colony in that region. There was great difference of opinion on this subject, and the leaders of the enterprise, and the principal persons in London whom they relied upon to furnish them with funds, were long in coming to a decision. Some had been in favor of going to Guiana, in South America, which, as it was in a tropical region, abounded with fruits and other natural productions, and enjoyed a continual summer throughout the year. Others were in favor of New England, on account of the very profitable fisheries off the coast in that quarter, which, then as now, were greatly resorted to. Others still, and the opinion of these last prevailed, preferred to go farther to the south, and yet not to pass beyond the jurisdiction of their own government. So they decided to apply to the Council of the London, or, as it was then often called, the Virginia Company.

After a long and tedious negotiation, during which many letters passed to and fro, and much discussion was held on various points of detail, a regular patent, or letter of authority, was granted to them to establish their colony in Southern Virginia. This document, however, was never of any service to them—inasmuch, as it turned out in the end, that they did not go to Southern Virginia at all.

THE QUESTION OF FUNDS

During the time while these negotiations were going on with the government, and with the London Company, the agents of the colonists were also engaged in maturing plans for raising the necessary funds. Of course, a considerable amount of money would be required. There would be vessels to be purchased, to carry the emigrants across the sea, and stores of all kinds to be provided, not merely for the voyage, but also to supply the infant colony after their arrival, during the time while the crops in their new fields were growing and ripening. It was necessary, also, to carry over various kinds of materials for their houses, such as glass, hinges, locks, latches, and other such things; and stuffs of different kinds for clothing, and also medicines. The colonists too, would require a large supply of tools and implements of various kinds, both for the cultivation of the ground and for mechanical work, and a complete provision of fishing-tackle, and a supply of guns and gunpowder, not only as a means of defending themselves from the Indians in case of necessity, and of destroying wild beasts, but also for the purpose of hunting game, in case they should find animals in the woods that were suitable for food.

Now, the question was, where the money necessary for all these purposes was to come from.

A JOINT STOCK COMPANY PROPOSED

The colonists themselves possessed very little money of their own. Nearly all the property which they once possessed, had been wasted away by the losses and the expenses which they had incurred, and very little now remained to most of them, except their household furniture, and some few implements of trade, and these things they intended to take with them. So it was concluded to form, what is called, a joint stock company, that is to say, an association of persons, to include, besides those who were to go to America and found the colony, others who were willing to contribute money to the enterprise, with the view of receiving a share in the profits that might be made, without emigrating themselves. There were several persons, merchants and others, in London, who seemed to be willing to do this, provided that the terms and conditions could be satisfactorily arranged.

TERMS OF SUBSCRIPTION TO THE STOCK PROPOSED BY THE COMPANY

The plan which the colonists authorized their agent to propose in London, was as follows. They set the value of the shares in the Joint Stock Company at ten pounds, which is equivalent to about fifty dollars. Every person over sixteen years of age, who should go out with the colony, and remain in America as a settler, should be entitled to one share, in consideration of his services, and every person who should contribute ten pounds in money, without going, should be entitled to the same. Of course, any person might take a number of shares, if he chose, by paying ten pounds for each; and if any colonist, besides going himself, were to contribute money, or furnish stores or provisions to any amount, he was to be entitled to extra shares, on that account, at the rate of one share for every ten pounds so furnished.

There were special arrangements for emigrants under sixteen years of age, and some other details not necessary to be specified here.

The shares being thus allotted, the business of the colony was then to be carried on for seven years, in common, except that each colonist was to have two days each week to work for himself and his own family, exclusively, and he was also to be allowed to hold his own house and garden, as his private property. All the other lands, and all property of every kind, owned or acquired by the colony, were to be kept in common until the end of seven years, and then the whole amount was to be divided among all the shareholders, in proportion to the number of shares which stood in their names.

These were the terms which the company in Leyden were prepared to offer to any persons in London, who might be disposed to contribute money to assist in carrying out the undertaking.

Terms Insisted on by the Contributors

These terms would seem to have been sufficiently liberal, but when the agents in London came to the point of actually receiving the subscriptions, and collecting the money from those who had given them encouragement that they would subscribe, they encountered serious difficulties. Some were dissatisfied because the company had decided not to go to Guiana. Others, because they were not going to New England, where they thought they could make a great deal of money by fishing. Others concluded, when the time for deciding arrived, that the whole enterprise was too uncertain, and that they would not risk their money. There were a few that remained, who said they would take shares, on condition that the two reservations which the colonists had made, namely, the house and garden for each settler, and two days each week for his own private purposes, should be given up, and that all the property and all the avails of labor of every kind, should be held in common, to be divided at the end of seven years among those concerned, in proportion to the number of shares owned by each. The agents, finding that they could not obtain funds in any other way, were obliged to accede to these terms.

Disappointment and Discontent of the Congregation

When the agents returned to Leyden, and reported to the congregation what they had done, those who had made up their minds to go to America were greatly disappointed and disheartened at the hard conditions which were exacted of them. To have all the avails of the labor of an emigrant for seven years, reckoned only as a counterpoise to a contribution of ten pounds, by a person remaining at home, seemed to them very discouraging. Even with the reservation of a homestead for each, and of two days' labor in the week for themselves, the conditions appeared to be sufficiently onerous, and many declared that they would not submit to this additional exaction. Some censured the principal agent for consenting to such terms; but he said, in reply, that it was not a matter of choice with him, but necessity. On no other conditions could he procure the money absolutely necessary for the outfit of the expedition. There was no alternative, he said, but for them to submit to those terms or to abandon the enterprise altogether.

The Final Decision

After much anxious deliberation, accompanied with very earnest and fervent prayer to Almighty God, to guide and direct them in their own perplexity, it was at length decided that a portion of the congregation should go. The amount of money which had been raised was not sufficient to provide for the emigration of the whole company at once. A selection was accordingly made of those who were either better able than the rest to sustain the fatigues and exposures of such an enterprise, or were more courageous and resolute in respect to undertaking it, and the preparations were immediately commenced for their departure.

The *Speedwell* and the *Mayflower*

Two vessels were procured for the voyage, the *Speedwell* and the *Mayflower*. Both were very small, the *Speedwell* being of about sixty tons, and the *Mayflower* of one hundred and eighty. The *Mayflower* was bought in London. The *Speedwell* was procured in Holland, and was to be employed in the first instance, in taking the whole company of emigrants over to England, to the port of Southampton, where the *Mayflower,* sent round from London, was to await them.

Leyden itself is not upon the sea, and the *Speedwell* was to come to Delft Haven, a port about fourteen miles distant from that town. Thither the party of emigrants repaired, accompanied by many of those who were to be left behind, and there took place the most solemn and affecting scene of the first embarkation.

"When they came to the place," says the eyewitness who described the scene, "they found the ship and all things ready. That night was spent with little sleep by the most, but with friendly entertainment and Christian discourse, and other real expressions of true Christian love. The next day, the weather being fair, they went on board, and their friends with them, when truly doleful was the sight of that sad and mournful parting; to see what sighs and sobs and prayers did sound amongst them; what tears did gush from every eye, and pithy speeches pierced each other's heart; so that sundry of the Dutch strangers, that stood on the quay as spectators, could not refrain from tears.

"But the tide, which stays for no man, calling them away that were thus loth to depart, their reverend pastor, falling down on his knees, and they all with him, with watery cheeks commended them, with most fervent prayers, to the Lord and his blessing—and then, with mutual embraces and many tears, they took their leave of one another."

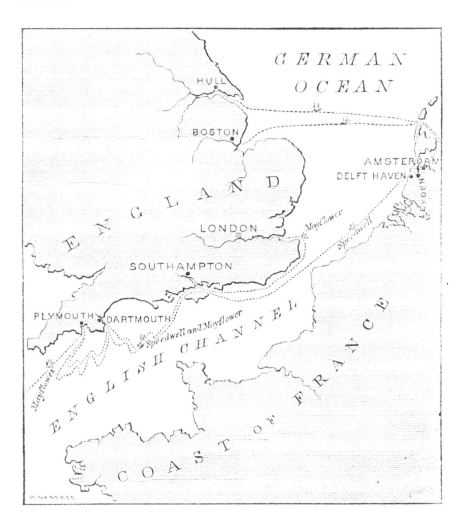

The Pastor's Farewell

As has already been intimated, Mr. Robinson himself did not accompany this first expedition. As only a minority of the church were to go at this time, it was thought best that the pastor should remain with the major portion until the time should come for them to follow. He came to Delft Haven to take leave of the company in person there, when they sailed from Holland. He also wrote a long letter of farewell, to be read to them just before their embarkation at Southampton. Accordingly, when everything was ready for their departure, the whole company were called together at an appointed time, and, at the meeting thus held, the letter was read to them, in connection with religious exercises appropriate to the occasion.

The letter was filled with earnest expressions of the affectionate attachment felt for them by their pastor, and the most heartfelt invocations of the blessing of God upon them, in the dangers and trials to which they were about to be exposed. It contained, also, many solemn counsels and earnest warnings to guard against the temptations and snares which would beset them on their way.

The reading of the letter produced a very deep and solemn impression upon all who heard it.

The Expedition Sails

The preparations and arrangements at Southampton occupied nearly a fortnight, and, at length, on the fifth of August, the two vessels set sail—the *Mayflower,* which was much the largest of the two vessels, commanded by Captain Jones, and the *Speedwell* by Captain Reynolds. The course of the vessels lay down Southampton Water to the Solent, thence between the Isle of Wight and the mainland out into the Channel, and so down the Channel, along the southern coast of England, toward the sea.

Difficulty with the *Speedwell*

The two vessels went along slowly on this course for several days, and then Captain Reynolds of the *Speedwell* began to complain that his vessel was leaky, and the indications of unsoundness in her were so alarming, he said, that he did not think it safe to proceed. So it was determined to go into port somewhere, and have the vessel examined. The nearest and most convenient port was Dartmouth, and there the two vessels put in.

THE DELAY AT DARTMOUTH

The *Speedwell* was taken to the dock at Dartmouth, and thoroughly examined, but the carpenters said they could not find that there was anything seriously at fault in her. She *ought* not to leak, for anything that they could discover. They however made some repairs upon her, and caulked her seams, and then delivered her to the charge of the captain again, giving it as their opinion that she was safe and sound for the voyage. So the company went on board, and the two vessels set sail again. They had been detained by the examination and repairs just a week.

The loss of this week was greatly regretted by all, inasmuch as, in consequence of preceding delays, they were already far behind their proper time. The summer was passing away, and there was danger of their not reaching their destination before the cold and stormy season of the year should set in. This made them very anxious, for it seemed to them that without some weeks of good weather after their arrival, they could not possibly make preparations for winter.

FINAL FAILURE OF THE *SPEEDWELL*

The expedition sailed from Dartmouth on the twenty-first of August, and after going on for several days longer, during which time the accounts of the performance of the *Speedwell* were looked for with the greatest interest and anxiety every day, by all on board both vessels, the company was at length greatly disheartened and discouraged by the report from Captain Reynolds that the vessel still leaked so badly, whenever the sea was rough, that he was convinced it was wholly unsafe to proceed in her. In case of a storm, nothing could prevent her taking in so much water that she would founder, and all on board perish.

So it was determined to make for a port again, and this time the place of refuge was Plymouth.[1] Here the *Speedwell* was again thoroughly examined. The workmen still could not find any leaks, nor any serious marks of injury or decay. So they concluded that the difficulty was a general weakness of the hull of the vessel, and that no alternative was left but to abandon her, and so make their voyage as well as they could with the *Mayflower* alone, though this would necessarily derange all their plans.

EXPLANATIONS OF THE MYSTERY

Two explanations were afterward given of this secret and mysterious leaking of the *Speedwell*. In the first place, the vessel did actually leak, as the captain alleged, and the difficulty was owing, as it afterward appeared, to her being too heavily masted. When the masts in any vessel, and the rigging which they sustain, are too heavy for the hull, the strain which is caused by the weight, in heavy weather, opens the seams, as the vessel rolls from side to side, in such a manner as to admit a great deal of water; and yet, when the vessel is still, as in the case of her arrival in port, the seams close up again, and the cause of the leakage entirely disappears. The masts in this case were afterward changed, and then the vessel did very well.

Besides this, the captain of the vessel had become discouraged and alarmed, and he wished to give up the voyage. This led him to exaggerate the danger, and to represent the leakage and unseaworthiness of the vessel as greater than it really was. The result of all was that, by common consent, it was determined to give up the *Speedwell,* and to make the voyage with the *Mayflower* alone. The provisions and stores, therefore, and as many of the passengers as it was safe to take, were transshipped. The remainder of the passengers were sent back to London, there to await another opportunity of prosecuting the voyage.

The whole number of emigrants that finally embarked on board the *Mayflower,* at Plymouth, was one hundred. It was on the sixth of September that they set sail.

---

[1]See map, on page 47.

The Voyage of the Mayflower

THE VOYAGE

Plymouth, as will be seen by the map, is near the Chops of the Channel, and the *Mayflower* soon after this, her final departure from port, came out into the broad and boundless ocean. The company on board enjoyed favoring winds and fair weather for a time, but at length the September gales came on, and the ship encountered so many contrary winds and fierce storms, that her frame was greatly shaken, and the upper works were made so leaky, that the berths and cabins were drenched with water. One of the main beams too, across the middle of the ship, began to bend and crack under the repeated and heavy strains which the vessel sustained, until the people really feared that the vessel could not finish the voyage, and a serious consultation was held between Captain Jones and the principal passengers, to determine whether it was not best to return to England.

It happened, however, that one of the passengers had a large iron screw among his effects—one which he had brought from Holland—and by means of this screw the carpenters contrived to bring the broken beam to its bearings again, and to secure it there by the proper fastenings, so that it seemed safe to go on.

They accordingly went on, but they continued to encounter many boisterous storms, so that for many days together, they could carry no sail, but lay almost at the mercy of the winds and waves. At length, however, after many weeks of slow and toilsome progress over adverse and stormy seas, to their unbounded joy, they heard the cry of land. The part of the coast which first came into view, was Cape Cod. They made the land on the ninth of November, having been more than two months at sea.

APPROACHING THE LAND

Of course, the whole company on board were overwhelmed with joy at the sight of land. They seemed too, to have been much pleased with the aspect of the shore, which was everywhere covered with trees, even down to the margin of the water. The women and children, who were by this time well-nigh worn out by the hardships,

51

privations, and exposures of the voyage, resulting not only from the cold and stormy weather, but also from their extremely crowded condition on board the ship, were very impatient to land.

But the place which had been decided upon for the settlement was the Hudson River, many leagues south of Cape Cod, and so the vessel was steered to the southward along the coast in that direction.

But the weather was cold and the wind was high, and that night another storm arose. Of course, the mariners had no chart or pilot to guide them, and as darkness came on, the vessel became entangled among shoals and islands, where the howling of the winds, and the roaring of the surf and breakers, were so appalling, that by common consent it was determined to proceed no further. So the vessel was beaded to the northward, and the next day, passing round the extremity of the cape, they made their way into a little bay where the water, landlocked, and sheltered, was smooth, and there the storm-tossed *Mayflower* was at length at rest.

CHAPTER IV
LANDING AT PLYMOUTH

The Harbor

The harbor into which the *Mayflower* entered was that of Provincetown, which is situated near the extremity of Cape Cod, and on the western side of it, where, as is seen upon the map, the land seemed to reach out a long arm to receive them, and to shelter them with its hand. It was on the eleventh of November, that the vessel came to anchor.

Explanation of Map

The map on the following page represents the place of the first anchorage, and the scene of the preliminary explorations and expeditions made by the company, as they will hereafter be described.

References

a Anchorage of the *Mayflower*.
bb First expedition on land.
cc First expedition in the shallop.
dd Second expedition in the shallop.
ee Expedition in search of the lost boy.

Condition of the Emigrants

The condition of the company on board the vessel as they came into port, was very forlorn. They were all greatly weakened and exhausted by the fatigues of the voyage, and their health was more or less impaired by the use of salt provisions and other hard sea fare to which they had so long been confined. They were somewhat

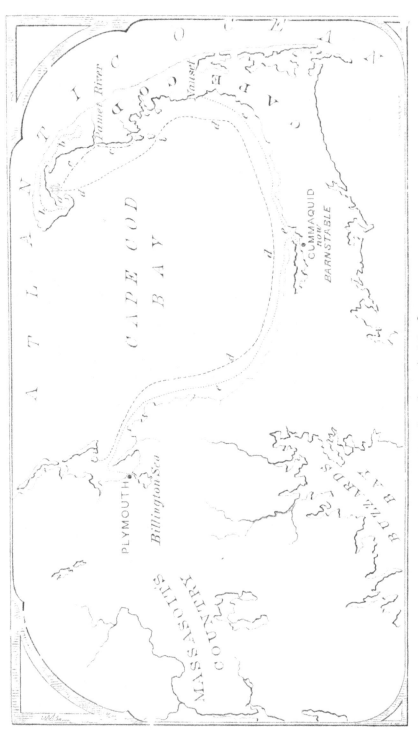

Landing from the Mayflower.

disheartened and discouraged too, by the prospects before them. They were obliged to stop and make their landing in a much colder and more inhospitable region than they had intended, and they were two months later in time than they had hoped to be, when leaving Leyden. Some of the men were discontented and uneasy under this state of things, and seemed inclined to find fault, and to make complaints, which threatened to cause difficulty.

IMPORTANT MEASURE RESOLVED UPON

These threatening appearances made the leading men quite anxious, and in order the better to bind the whole company together they drew up a solemn agreement, by which they formed themselves into a body politic, and agreed to submit faithfully to such rules and regulations as should be made, by common consent, for the good of all.

This document has since become quite famous, as the first example in the history of mankind, of the foundation of a civil state, by a written constitution, on the basis of universal suffrage. The document was as follows:—

THE FIRST CONSTITUTION

In the name of God, Amen. We whose names are underwritten, the loyal subjects of our dread sovereign lord, King James, by the grace of God, of Great Britain, France, and Ireland, King, Defender of the Faith, &c., having undertaken for the glory of God, and advancement of the Christian faith, and honor of our king and country, a voyage to plant the first colony in the northern parts of Virginia, do by these presents solemnly and mutually, in the presence of God and of one another, covenant and combine ourselves together, into a civil body politic, for our better ordering and preservation, and furtherance of the ends aforesaid; and by virtue hereof to enact, constitute, and frame such just and equal laws, ordinances, acts, constitutions and offices, from time to time, as shall be thought most meet and convenient for the public good of the colony, unto which we promise all due submission and obedience.

In witness whereof, we have hereunder subscribed our names, at Cape Cod; the 11th of November, in the year of the reign of our sovereign lord, King James, of England, France, and Ireland, the 18th, and of Scotland the 54th, Anno Domini, 1620.

This document was signed by all the men, forty in number, each one placing opposite his name the number of persons in his family. The whole number of persons amounted to one hundred and one. These were the founders of New England, and this document was the origin and precursor of the many democratic constitutions that have since been established in the Northern States of America, by which civil government is recognized, not as a hereditary estate of power and prerogative in the hands of a few, but as a practical business, to be transacted for the common good, under the direction and control of all whose interests are involved in it.

At the same time that this constitution was adopted, the colonists chose one of their number to be their first governor, under it. His name was John Carver. He had been one of the agents employed in the preliminary negotiations at London, and had performed his duties in a very able and efficient manner. He lived, however, to hold the office of governor only a short time.

LANDING ON THE CAPE

As soon as the *Mayflower* was at anchor in the harbor at Provincetown, everybody was eager to land. The deck was crowded with men, women, and children, all gazing with intense interest on the scene around them. A boat was sent on shore to procure wood and water. Many of the passengers went on shore too—though the weather was freezing cold. And what made it worse, the water shoaled so gradually from the beach, that the boat grounded long before it reached the land, and the people were obliged to wade some distance through the water. Notwithstanding these difficulties a great many of the passengers insisted on going to the land, and

Laying the foundations.

a considerable number of them took colds in consequence of the exposure, and were made quite sick by them. Some of them never recovered from the coughs thus induced, but fell into consumptions and died in the course of the winter. These terrible results were due undoubtedly to the feeble and exhausted condition the people were in, in consequence of the bad air, and unwholesome food, and close confinement, which they had endured on board the ship, and by which their health had been so much impaired that they were wholly unfitted to sustain even ordinary exposures.

Whales

They saw from time to time numbers of whales playing about in the water of the harbor, and bay, and this sight was extremely tantalizing to the master of the vessel, Captain Jones, and to his crew, who said that if they had only brought harpoons with them, they could have taken whales enough to load their vessel with oil, by which means they might have made their fortunes.

A Reconnoitering Party

One of the first things done, after the vessel was made secure at her moorings, was to send an armed reconnoitering party, of fifteen or sixteen men, to make an excursion of a few hours into the interior, to see what they could find. This party were to examine the lay of the land, by ascending some eminence from which they could obtain a general view, and also to observe the productions of the soil, and especially to ascertain whether any traces of inhabitants could be perceived.

The party returned at night, bringing with them a boatload of cedars, or junipers, as they called them, for firewood. They had ascended a hill from which they could see across to the ocean on the outside of the cape, and could also trace the line of the coast for some distance to the southward.

They found the woods full of oaks, pines, sassafras, juniper, birches, holly trees, vines, ash, and walnut trees, and many others. They dug down too, in some places through the sand, which lay upon the top of the ground, and found a layer of good, rich, black earth below, which they considered a very encouraging token.

They saw no signs, however, that the land was inhabited. There were no dwellings of any kind to be found, nor roads, nor paths, nor any other indications whatever of the presence or agency of human beings.

The Shallop

In the meantime, preparations began to be made for a more extended exploring tour along the neighboring shores, by means of a boat, in order to select a place for making a settlement. The captain of the vessel urged the emigrants to press forward this business as fast as possible, for it was getting very late for him to return to England; and besides, the longer he and his crew remained on the coast, the more the common stock of provisions would be consumed. As it was, they had only a very limited supply.

The boat, in which this excursion was to be made, was the shallop, a pretty large boat, fitted with masts and sails. It was found, when they came to put this boat on board at Southampton, that it would not go in under the deck without being cut down, and all the voyage it had been used as a sleeping place for several of the women, and as a place of storage for baggage; and under the rough usage to which it had thus been subjected it had become very much out of repair. The crew hoisted it up, however, upon the deck, and then contrived to float it to the shore—and there the carpenter and his mates were set at work rebuilding it, as it were, and making it ready for service.

Miles Standish's Expedition

While the carpenter and his men were thus engaged in getting the shallop ready, some of the more courageous and resolute of the men proposed to make an excursion of two or three days, on foot, along the coast to the southward. This was thought to be a very hazardous undertaking, as such a party could carry but very little food with them, in addition to the weight of their arms; and they would have no means of retreat or escape, in case of an attack from

Indians, or of any accident. Still, as the men were very earnest to go, the governor consented.

The leading man in this proposal was a colonist, named Miles Standish. He was a man of small size, but of great bodily vigor, and of indomitable courage and perseverance. So the party was organized, and Miles Standish was made the captain of it. Three other persons were appointed as his counselors, to give him their aid and advice, when necessary. The whole party consisted of sixteen. Each man was armed with a sword and musket, and wore also a steel corslet, to protect his body from the arrows of the Indians. They also had ammunition to carry, and food for two days. Thus they were all very heavily loaded.

It was arranged that they were to be out two nights only, and on the second day they were to come down to the shore, and build a fire there, so that the people on board the ship could see the smoke of it, and know that all was well.

Departure of the Expedition

It was on Wednesday, the fifteenth of November, that the party set forth. The men were put on shore by one of the small boats. They immediately commenced their march, moving in single file along the beach to the southward. The company on board watched them as long as they continued in sight. At length, however, they turned around a point of land and disappeared from view.

After proceeding about a mile or more, they saw before them a company of men on the shore, though they were at too great a distance to be clearly distinguished. They supposed that these were persons belonging to the ship, as there were one or two parties that had gone on shore that morning, and were now somewhere on the land. On drawing nearer, however, they perceived that the men they saw were Indians, and that they had a dog with them. The Indians, as soon as they discovered the strangers, made off at once into the woods, whistling the dog after them. Captain Standish and his men followed; but the Indians ran on at great speed, so that, heavily loaded as the English were, they could not overtake them. They persevered, however, in the attempt, following the Indians by the tracks they made, for miles, hoping to find their encampment. But night at length came on, and they were obliged to give up the pursuit. So they gathered some wood, and built a fire, and after eating their supper they lay down in the bushes near the fire for the night, having first set three sentinels at three different points a little way from the fire to keep watch.

They felt considerable apprehension that they might be attacked by the Indians during the night, but they were not disturbed.

THE SECOND DAY

The second day the party continued their march, and they met with quite a variety of adventures. They followed the track of the Indians for some distance, but could not find their dwellings, and at length they got entangled among bushes and briers, so that they became sadly scratched and torn, and, what was worse than all, they could not find any springs or streams of water, and thus they came very near perishing of thirst. At length, however, they came to a little dell, in the bottom of which they found some springs, "of which," says one of them in his account, "we were heartily glad, and sat down and drank our first New England water with as much delight as we ever drunk drink in all our lives."

INDIAN DISCOVERIES

After this, they went on very much refreshed, and with new courage. They turned first toward the shore, where they made a great fire as a signal to those on board the vessel, which was now, perhaps, ten or twelve miles distant from them, but yet in such a position that the smoke could be seen. Then they turned into the interior again, and, in the course of the day, they discovered many traces of the Indians. Among other things, they found some curious looking mounds, which they dug into a little way, and found old bows and arrows, and other such things within, which led them to think that the mounds were graves—and so they filled them up again, after having first replaced everything carefully as they had found it.

A Treasure Found

At length they came to a place where there seemed once to have been a hut of some kind, and near it was an iron kettle, which had evidently come from a European ship. There were some old boards, too, lying by, which indicated that the hut had been built by shipwrecked mariners.

Near this place was a fresh looking mound, which seemed to have been just made, and the party determined to explore it more thoroughly. They accordingly stationed sentinels all around, and then began to dig. It was very easy digging, for the mound was made of loose sand. After digging down a little way they found, among some other things, a deposit which they considered a great prize. It was a large narrow necked basket, well made and new, and filled with *fresh Indian corn,* some of it on the ears, with kernels of mixed colors, yellow, red, and blue, on the same cob. The basket held three or four bushels.

They were very desirous to take away this corn, as they wanted it for seed, but they had great doubts whether it would be right for them to do so. Finally, they concluded to take the kettle, and as much of the corn as they could carry away, and afterward, if they could find the Indians that the property belonged to, they would give them back the kettle, and pay them liberally for the corn.

So they filled the kettle with the loose corn, and gave it to two men to carry by means of a pole. The other men took the ears, and also filled their pockets with the loose corn. The rest of the corn they put back into the basket, and buried it again, basket and all, just as they found it.

After this, they wandered on, making other similar discoveries, until at length, when the sun went down, they came to a halt near a freshwater pond, where they built a great fire and encamped for the night. It was cold and rainy, and the wind was so high that they were obliged to build a barricade of bushes to the windward of the fire, in order to shelter themselves from the cold.

THE THIRD DAY

On the third day the party turned their faces homeward. They got lost in the woods, however, on the way, and suffered much from the cold and the wet. As they were wandering about in the thickets they came in one place to a trap, which the Indians had set, to catch deer. It was made by bending down the top of a stout young sapling, and securing it to a stake by means of a rope and a noose, in such a manner that any animal coming near, and attempting to eat the acorns which were put under it for bait, would get caught in the noose, and be pulled up into the air, by the elastic force of the sapling. While the men were examining this trap, one of them incautiously came too near, so as to spring it, and got caught in it by the leg, and the others were obliged to hold down the sapling and release him.

At length, after many devious wanderings, during which sometimes they had to scramble through thickets of thorns, and sometimes to wade up to their knees in the ice cold water of the creeks and inlets, the men succeeded in making their way back, weary and wayworn, to the shore opposite the vessel, where they fired a gun for a signal, and Captain Jones sent a boat and brought them all on board.

EXPEDITION IN THE SHALLOP

In about ten days after this, the shallop was ready, and a party was organized to go on an expedition in her. The shallop was quite a large sailboat, and the object of the expedition was to explore the mouths of the rivers along the coast, with a view of finding a place for the settlement. A small boat was to go with the shallop, for the purpose of examining inlets and shallow bays. Captain Jones was placed in command of the expedition. He took with him ten of his own men—that is, of the crew of the vessel—to manage the sails of the shallop, and to row the small boat. Besides these, twenty-four of the colonists—more than half of the men—and all thoroughly armed, were to be of the party.

The expedition thus organized set sail, proceeding along the coast to the southward. But the weather proved to be extremely unfavorable for the work undertaken. It was very cold, and soon a snowstorm came on, which not only made it impossible for the party to keep the sea, but also interfered greatly with their making any examinations on land, as the ground soon became covered with several inches of snow.

Still they persevered. They entered the mouths of the rivers, and explored the banks of them; and often went on shore to examine the country, and see if they could find any traces of inhabitants. They found the same mound which Miles Standish had discovered, and opened it again so as to procure the rest of the corn. They also found several other similar mounds, and from them they obtained more corn, until at length they procured a sufficient supply for seed for the next spring. They also procured a quantity of beans, and wheat, and some other things of value to them.

The Frost

They found great difficulty in digging into the mounds which contained these things, on account of the frost. The ground was frozen several inches deep, and as they had brought with them no suitable tools for breaking through this crust, the only thing they could do was to cut through it first by means of their swords and cutlasses, until they had made a hole large enough to put in the end of a lever, by means of which the frozen part of the ground could be broken up, after which the digging became comparatively easy.

Embalmed Bodies

In one of the mounds they came upon two bodies—one that of a man, and the other that of a little child, both of which seemed to have been, in a certain degree, embalmed by means of a very fragrant red powder in which the bodies were enveloped. The flesh was nearly all decayed. The hair, on the skull of the man, was of a yellow color, which made the party think that it must have been the body of a European, since the hair of Indians is always black. Besides, the body was dressed in a sailor's canvas jacket, and in cloth trousers. And yet the interment had evidently been made by Indians, as everything was arranged in the Indian manner, and the grave contained, besides the bodies, a great many implements and ornaments of Indian manufacture. There were, however, also some objects which were evidently of European origin, such as a knife, a sail-needle, and some iron things. Around the legs and arms of the child were bound bracelets of wampum, such as the Indians use, and also a little bow, which had apparently belonged to the boy when he was alive.

The men took out some of the most curious of the implements and trinkets found in this grave, and putting the rest back carefully, they covered everything up again as before. They came to the conclusion that the man buried here was some European captive that the Indians had taken from the crew of a vessel that had been wrecked, perhaps, upon the coast, and who had contrived to make himself a person of distinction among them.

INDIAN HOUSES

In the course of their explorations, the party came in one place to some Indian huts or wigwams, though there were no inhabitants in them. The houses were made of long and slender poles, with both ends of each pole planted in the ground, in holes forming a circle, in such a manner that the poles made the framework of a dome. This framework was covered with mats outside, for the roof, an opening being left in the center for the smoke to go out. There was a place for a fire in the center of the hut within, with crotched sticks on each side, and a cross-bar above to hang the kettle upon. All around there were mats spread upon the ground, and close under the roof were stored many utensils of various kinds—such as wooden bowls, trays and dishes, earthen pots, baskets of various sorts, some made of shells and others of wickerwork. Some of these last were very pretty, with different colors interwoven.

There were also in the different huts various trophies of the chase—the feet and horns of deer, eagles' claws, and other such things. There were some articles of food, too, such as baskets of roasted acorns, dried fish, and some broiled herring; and supplies of materials for making baskets and mats, consisting of bundles of flags, coarse grass, and bulrushes.

In a word, the huts seemed to be completely furnished, and well stocked with stores, as if in the actual occupancy of Indian families. And yet no inhabitants were to be seen.

TAKING A LIBERTY

Our party of visitors took the liberty to select from all these things in the huts whatever they thought would be of any service to them, and to carry them away. They admitted to themselves that they had, strictly speaking, no right to do this; but they quieted their consciences on this point by forming and declaring an intention to come back the next day, with a supply of beads, and other such things as Indians are pleased with, and to leave them in the houses by way of payment in barter for what they had taken. This excellent intention, however, they did not have an opportunity to carry out, and so the poor Indians, when they came back to their homes, found that somebody had been there, and had robbed them of the most valuable portion of their household goods.

It ought to be added, however, that some months after this, when the colonists had become established in Plymouth, they made full compensation to the Indians, so far as they were able, for all the property which they had taken from them in these irregular ways.

A DEBATE

As soon as this first expedition in the shallop returned, there arose a great debate in respect to what should be done. The chief place which the shallop party had explored was the mouth of the Pamet River, a small river which flows into the sea, on the western side of the cape, in this region; and some were in favor of searching no longer, but at once fixing upon that spot as the place of their settlement. Others thought it best to look farther. There were a great many arguments both for and against the plan—and at last it was decided to make one more examination of the land, and that, on the other side of the bay, toward the southeast. Accordingly, the shallop was fitted out once more, and, on the sixth of December, which was nearly a week after the return of the first expedition, she sailed again.

BABY BORN

About this time an event occurred on board the *Mayflower,* as she lay in the harbor of Cape Cod, which produced a great excitement among all the party—an excitement, too, of quite a novel kind—and that was, a baby was born. The baby was a boy—the son of one of the colonists named White. They named him Peregrine. Notwithstanding the scenes of suffering and hardship, among which he made his entrance into the world, he seems to have been a healthy child, for he lived more than eighty years. When he was about forty-five years of age, the colony made a grant to him of two hundred acres of land, in consideration of his having been the first child born in New England.

SAILING OF THE SECOND EXPEDITION

It was a bitter cold day when the second expedition in the shallop set out. It consisted of eighteen persons in all, twelve being colonists, among whom were several of the principal men, and six officers and seamen belonging to the vessel. The day was Wednesday, the sixth of December. There was a high wind blowing on the day of the departure of the expedition, and it set them directly toward a point of land which projected into the sea, near the vessel, so that they had to toil long and arduously at the oars, in order to clear the sands and shoals around it. During this time several of the men were very sick, and the sea, which dashed over them, froze upon their clothes, making them as stiff as if the men had been dressed in iron mail. At length they weathered the point, and got somewhat under the protection of the land beyond, and so sailed along the western shore of the cape toward the southward, exploring every opening which seemed likely to lead to an inlet from the sea which might serve them for a harbor.

DIVISION OF THE PARTY

On the morning of the second day they divided the party, one half going on shore to explore the land, while the remainder continued in the shallop, following the coast. The two parties did not meet again till night. For several hours they lost sight of each other, and all suffered no little anxiety, lest they should not succeed in finding each other again. During the day both parties observed the bodies of grampuses, which had been entangled by the ice, and driven up upon the shore by the waves. These animals would have afforded them a fine supply of oil, if they had had the means of securing it, and the necessary time to spare.

They also saw some Indians before them on the beach, occupied about something black, though they could not see what it was. As soon as the Indians saw them, they ran off into the woods, and when the English came to the spot they found that the black thing was a grampus, which the Indians were cutting up.

A Midnight Alarm

The party on land, fortunately, toward night, discovered the boat, and coming down to the shore, they made signals, and the shallop came to them. That night they encamped on the land, securing the shallop to the shore nearby, and setting a watch. In the middle of the night there was an alarm. The sentinels heard some sort of noise, and shouted out, "Arm! arm!" so vociferously as to arouse the whole camp in an instant. At the same time they fired two or three guns at random, for the purpose of frightening the enemy. Presently, all became still again, and they supposed that the noise had been made by wolves or foxes, or some other wild animals prowling through the woods.

An Attack by the Indians

The next morning, when they were breaking up their camp, and preparing to embark again on board the shallop, they were suddenly attacked by a large party of Indians. They had already embarked a considerable portion of their effects on board the shallop, and had laid the rest, including their arms, on the beach, ready to be put on board, and about half the number had gone back to the place of the encampment, which was a little way inland, under the trees, in order to bring down what articles remained there, when suddenly a most awful yell burst upon the ears of all the party. It was the Indian war-whoop; and, as it came from forty or fifty voices, the sound was truly terrific. At the same moment a shower of arrows came flying in from the thickets in every direction around. Then ensued a scene of the direst terror and confusion—the men on the shore rushing down to the beach for the guns, and the two parties, those on the land and in the boats, calling to each other, and shouting out directions and orders. Providentially, no one was wounded by the arrows, and as soon as the men recovered their arms the Indians fled. They pursued them a quarter of a mile, and then, firing two or three muskets after them, they gave up the chase and came back to the shallop.

They picked up *eighteen* arrows which had been shot at them, and put them into the shallop. These arrows were afterward sent to England, when the *Mayflower* returned.

DIFFICULTIES AND DISCOURAGEMENTS

The shallop went on to the southward, and so followed the coast round to the westward, the men looking out everywhere for some inlet where there might be promise of a harbor. But a storm came on, and the air was so filled with driving sleet and snow, that they could scarcely see the land. In consequence of this, they passed by Barnstable Harbor, which might have answered their purpose very well. They went on, therefore, anxiously looking out for some place of refuge. In the meantime, the wind and sea increased, until they were all in great danger. The rudder was carried off its hinges by the shocks given it by the seas, so that they had to steer with oars. After a time, the opening of Plymouth Harbor came into view, and they strained every nerve to get in. At length the pressure of the wind was so great upon the sail that the mast gave way, and came down over the side broken into three pieces, a perfect wreck.

Still they pressed on. Some seized the broken fragments of the mast and the entangled sails and rigging, and pulled them in on board. Others worked laboriously at the oars; others bailed out the water which every sea threw over the bows. Thus they struggled on, and, as very fortunately they were assisted by the tide, which, as it happened, was then setting in, they finally passed a projecting point of land, and soon afterward found themselves in smooth water, in Plymouth Harbor.

They landed on an island, which they afterward named Clark's Island, in honor of one of their number, the mate of the *Mayflower,* and which retains that name to this day. It was now Saturday night, and so they established an encampment on the shore, and remained there quietly that night and all the next day, intending to resume their labors on Monday morning.

They spent Monday in making excursions on the land. They found everything favorable there for their proposed settlement, and they determined to return at once to the *Mayflower* with the report of their discovery. They accordingly set sail on Tuesday, and, passing directly across the bay, reached the *Mayflower* at her anchorage at Provincetown that afternoon.

The report which they made was favorably received, and everybody began at once to make preparations for the sailing of the *Mayflower* across the bay. In two days the ship was ready, and on Friday she attempted the passage, but was driven back by contrary winds. On Saturday she succeeded in crossing the bay, and entering Plymouth Harbor in safety. The company remained on board during the Sabbath, and the next week they landed and took possession of their new home.

CHAPTER V
FIRST WINTER AT PLYMOUTH

CONDITION OF THE SETTLERS

When the *Mayflower* came to anchor in the harbor of Plymouth, and the colonists began to make preparations for their final landing, their situation was forlorn and discouraging in the extreme. The whole party were well-nigh worn-out with their protracted exposures and sufferings. Their long confinement on board ship, where they had suffered greatly from bad and insufficient food, and foul air, had brought on symptoms of scurvy, one of the most horrible of all diseases. Then the exposure to wet and cold which they had endured since their arrival on the coast, in the long and fatiguing excursions which they had made on the land—in their wadings through the water when going to and fro between the ship and the shore, and when passing creeks and morasses—and in sleeping at their encampments by open fires in the midst of storms of snow and rain, and with nothing to protect them but a barricade of bushes—had given a great many of them coughs and colds, which were now, in several cases, becoming incipient consumption. Four or five had already died. One man died on board the ship, in the harbor of Plymouth, before they landed. Several others were seriously sick, and many more were so weak and feeble that they could only move about with great difficulty, appearing more fit to be sent to a hospital than to go to work, in such winter weather, to clear land and build houses.

THEIR RESOLUTION AND FORTITUDE

Still they did not despair. They sent parties on shore to explore the country in the immediate vicinity of the harbor, with a view to selecting the spot where they should build their little town. These explorers found a great deal to encourage them; or rather, with the resolute and hopeful spirit which animated them, they contrived to educe a great deal of encouragement from the little that they found.

There were many wild fowl on the waters of the inlets and creeks, and the explorers came to the conclusion that there would be fish in the proper season. They discovered a navigable river emptying into the bay, and several running brooks of very sweet fresh water, which was very delicious to their taste after having been confined for so many weeks to the nauseous, stagnant liquid supplied by the tanks and water-casks of the vessel. They dug down in different places to examine the soil, and found a rich, black mould, which promised to be very fertile. They found, too, a considerable breadth of land which the Indians had cleared, and where corn had been planted. This was a very great advantage to them. Beyond these fields were woods where there grew a great variety of trees, which they thought would, in time, be very useful. One party reported that they saw "two or three great oaks, but not very thick, pines, walnuts, beech, ash, birch, hazel, holly, asp, sassafras in abundance, and vines everywhere, cherry trees, plum trees, and many others which we know not."

They found, too, sand and gravel, and excellent clay, not only such as was good for making bricks, but also for pottery.

These were the results of the first day's explorings, and when the various parties came back to the ship at night, wearied with their marching, and reported their discoveries, all on board took courage.

The Place of Settlement

These examinations of the country around the bay were continued for a day or two longer, and finally, on comparing the results, some difference of opinion arose in respect to the best place for the town. Some were in favor of building it on the island, on account of the greater safety of an insular position. They could watch against the Indians better, they said, if surrounded by water, and defend themselves more effectually. But then, the island was rough and rocky, and was covered with woods, so that no food could be raised upon it without first clearing the land, and this would be a work of immense labor and difficulty. Then there were no brooks or springs upon the island to furnish them with water. There were, it is true, at this season, some little ponds or pools here and there among the rocks, but it was thought probable that they would all dry up in the summer.

On the other hand, there was a place on the mainland where there was a great deal of ground already cleared, and where corn had evidently been planted a few years before, but which now appeared to be abandoned. Why it was thus abandoned was a mystery which was afterward explained. Near this place, too, was "a very sweet brook running under the hillside, and many delicate springs of excellent water." In a word, the question lay between the means of obtaining food, with danger from enemies, on one side, and security, with want, if not starvation, on the other. But it was too late now to shrink from danger; so it was decided, by a majority of voices, to go to the mainland. The decision was made after a solemn season of prayer, in which the whole company joined together in imploring the direction of Almighty God to guide them in the right way.

A STORM

This question was settled on Wednesday, the twentieth of December, according to their reckoning, which was by "old style." On the next morning a terrible storm arose, and continued to rage for several days with such violence as entirely to put a stop to all operations. A party of about twenty had been left on shore the night before, but the wind and sea were so high that for two days they could not be brought on board again, so that they were obliged to remain there all that time without shelter. The shallop contrived to get to the shore once during this time, to carry them provisions, otherwise they would have perished with hunger.

The vessel lay all this time at anchor, a mile and a half from the shore—that being as near as it was safe for her to come.

PREPARATIONS FOR BUILDING

As soon as the storm subsided, as many of the party as were well enough to make any active exertion, were sent on shore, and went vigorously to work, felling trees and hewing timber for the building. Their plan was, first of all, to build what they called their *common house,* which was intended to contain the stores from the ship, and also to furnish a shelter for the men while they were building houses for their families. This first building was to be twenty feet square. They proceeded very systematically with this work, dividing the men into gangs, some to fell trees, some to saw them into the proper lengths, some to split straight-grained logs into planks, and some to carry the logs and planks, when they were prepared, to the place where the building was to be erected. They continued this work for several days. They were frequently interrupted by fresh storms, and by alarms from the Indians. The sickness, too, was spreading, and one after another of the workmen was obliged to yield and give up the struggle. Still the rest persevered, until at length the building, which was made of logs and, as has already been stated, was about twenty feet square, was enclosed and roofed in, and was in a condition to afford shelter. A portion of the company, those namely that were most actively engaged in carrying on the work, from this time made this building their abode, though still far the greater portion of the company remained on board the ship.

LAYING OUT THE TOWN

As soon as the common house was far enough advanced to afford shelter, the company began to make arrangements for building the private dwellings. They prepared a list of all the families, making the number as small as possible, by combining such as could be combined, and assigning single persons to the families of the married men, as they could agree together. They found thus that all could be accommodated in nineteen houses. They then measured off the lots for these houses. It was necessary to have them as small as possible, and to put them all compactly together, so that it should not require too much work to enclose the whole in a stout palisade, necessary to defend the place from the Indians. The lots were made exceedingly small, in fact, being only about nine feet wide by fifty long. They were arranged side by side, in two rows, with a space for a street between. The houses, or huts, which they were going to build, would consequently have only nine feet front. The whole town, therefore, if town it may be called—common house, garden ground and all included—covered an area of only one hundred feet square. When these lots were measured and marked out, the company began, at the beginning, with a recognition of the democratic principle on which their whole enterprise was founded, by apportioning them among the different families *by lot,* and all the men prepared to go to work at once upon their dwellings.

THE FIRST SUNDAY ON SHORE

These preparations and arrangements were completed on Saturday night, December 30, according to their mode of reckoning, and Sunday, December 31, they considered their first Sabbath on shore, as it was the first that any portion of their number were able to spend under a permanent roof. They considered this day, therefore, the era of the establishment of their settlement, and they named the place Plymouth, in memory of the port at which they had taken their final farewell of their native land.

The mode of reckoning has since this time been changed from what is called the old style to the new, and this makes some confusion in attempting to compare these dates with those of the present day. It is also somewhat difficult to say which of the various days of their landing at Plymouth should be considered as best representing the first act of possession. The 22d of December was the day, however, which was fixed upon, at a very early period, as the day to be celebrated in commemoration of the event, and that day will probably continue to be honored as the anniversary of the landing of the Pilgrims at Plymouth, to the end of time.

THE FORT

In addition to the little village of houses above described, the colonists planned and constructed a sort of fort. It was built upon an elevation near their town, and consisted of a platform for guns, which were to be brought there from the vessel, and mounted in such a position as to command the surrounding approaches. This structure was not ready for several weeks after this time, so much were the labors of the company interrupted by the continued and increasing illness among the families, and by the cold, wet, and gloomy weather. When, however, at length the fort was ready, the captain and the crew of the *Mayflower* brought the heavy guns on shore, and the men, all taking hold together, dragged them up the hill and mounted them in their places.

Signs of the Indians

The company felt that these precautions were necessary, for they had abundant evidence that there were Indians all around them. They often saw the smokes made by their fires. Once or twice Captain Standish went out, with three or four others, to make a wide detour into the country, hoping to discover some of the natives. He found a number of deserted wigwams, but saw no Indians.

Indians had, however, actually been seen in some cases. One man, who was at work alone in the woods, hearing a noise as of something coming, ran and hid under some bushes and watched; and he saw twelve Indians go tramping by, in single file, stepping cautiously and stealthily one after the other, along the path.

At another time two men left their tools at a place in the woods where they had been at work, and came home to their dinner. On returning to the place the tools were gone. A party of Indians had carried them away.

The Military Company

In order to be prepared for any emergency that might arise, the colonists formed all the men capable of bearing arms into a military company, and chose Miles Standish for captain. While they were actually engaged in arranging this business, an incident occurred which reminded them that they were not attending to it any too soon, for they spied upon the top of a hill, over against the village, and about a quarter of a mile distant, two Indians who stood there making signs for them to come over. Miles Standish and another man, taking one gun with them, immediately went over, and before they got near to the Indians they laid down the gun and advanced unarmed toward the savages, holding up their empty hands in token of amity. But the Indians turned and ran off into the woods, where, as Miles Standish and his companion judged from the sounds they heard, there was a large party of their comrades waiting for them. Miles Standish and his companion waited for some time, but they could not induce the Indians to return, nor succeed in opening any communication with them.

Two Men Lost

At one time the whole company, both those on land and those who still remained on board the ship, were thrown into a state of great anxiety and alarm by the disappearance of two men, who strayed away into the woods and got lost, and so remained out all night, leading everyone to suppose that they had been seized, and perhaps massacred by the Indians.

These two men had been engaged, with some others, in cutting furze, with sickles, to make thatch for thatching their roofs. They had two dogs with them. After working together for a while, until they had cut nearly all the furze there was at that place, the two men, leaving the others to finish it, went on to another spot, taking the dogs with them, expecting the others to follow in a short time.

The men, thus left behind, finished their work, and then went on to the appointed place where their two companions were to await them—but when they came to the spot, there were neither men nor dogs to be seen. They hallooed and shouted, and went into the thickets all around, to search for them, but without success. They then returned to the settlement to report the story, and a party was sent out to try to find the missing men. This party came back at night without having gained any tidings of them—and the next morning a party of twelve were sent out, all well-armed, and supplied also with food for the lost men, in case they should be found. But they, too, came home without discovering any traces of them.

THE ADVENTURES OF THE LOST MEN

The truth was, that the two men had taken it into their heads to make a little excursion into the woods, beyond the place of rendezvous, to see what they could find. They came soon to the shore of a pond, where they saw a deer that had apparently come to drink. The dogs immediately gave chase to the deer, and the two men followed. Under the excitement of the chase they were led away farther than they intended, and when at length they attempted to return, they could not find the way. It was a cold and wet day, and the sky was clouded, so that they had no sun to guide them. They wandered about all the afternoon, and when night came on, they began to suffer greatly with cold and hunger. They had no warm garments—having come out clad only for work in the middle of the day—no food, and no weapons but their sickles. At length, when it became so dark that they could travel no longer, they lay down under some bushes, but were soon alarmed by a roaring noise, which they thought was made by two lions—for it was fully believed by everyone, at this time, that the woods in America were full of lions.

They started up and ran to the nearest tree, determined to climb up into it as soon as they should see the lions coming. They found, too, that the dogs were eager to rush at the supposed lions, and they were obliged to hold them back by main force. The alarm, however, proved to be false, for the noise of the roaring, whatever it might have been, soon died away. The men remained, nevertheless, at the foot of the tree, in the cold and snow, all night, and in a state of extreme anxiety and suffering.

The next morning, though scarcely able to stand, the men contrived to ascend an eminence, from which they obtained a distant view of the harbor, and thus found out which way they must go to reach home. It was so far, however, and they were so exhausted and lame, that they did not reach home until night. They were almost in a perishing condition when they arrived. The feet of one of them were so swollen from the effects of the frost, that he had to have his shoes cut off, and it was a long time before he was able to use his feet at all.

ALARMS OF FIRE

The chimneys put up by the settlers were of course very imperfect, and as the only means they had of making the roofs tight was covering them with a thatch of furze, the danger from fire was very great. In repeated instances these thatches took fire, and occasioned great alarm. At one time, early in the morning, before light, and while all the people within were in their beds, a spark caught in the thatch of the common house, and the roof was soon all of a blaze. The men on board the *Mayflower* were greatly alarmed at the sight of this fire, for they supposed the Indians had come, and attacked the company on shore, and were burning the buildings. They immediately set off for the shore to aid their comrades, but, on account of the distance of the vessel, and the lowness of the tide at that time, it was long before they could reach the land.

When, at length, they arrived on the spot, they found, greatly to their relief, that the fire had been the result of an accident, and was, moreover, now nearly extinguished. The thatch had been all burnt off the roof, but the roof itself, as well as the body of the building, having been made of green logs, resisted the fire, so that they succeeded in arresting it.

They were all greatly alarmed, however, and saw that they had narrowly escaped destruction. The building was crowded with people, the beds covering the floor as close together as they could stand, and many of the occupants were sick. There was also considerable gunpowder in the building, and in a greatly exposed condition, and a number of guns also, all loaded. In a word, the whole party had narrowly escaped a total and most terrible destruction. As it was, however, no other evil result followed than the necessity of procuring fresh furze, and thatching the roof again.

PROGRESS OF THE SICKNESS

A great many pages might be filled, if the space could be afforded, in narrating incidents like these, which occurred to diversify, so painfully, the experience of the colonists, during the months of January and February. The hardships, trials, and disasters, which they had to endure, were endlessly varied. But the great calamity of all, the one under the awful gloom and terror of which all other misfortunes seemed scarcely worthy of regard, was the continued sickness, and the dreadful mortality which resulted from it. The diseases, which the confinement, and the other privations endured by the company on board ship, during their voyage, and their subsequent exposures, during the time that they were beating about the bay, before their final landing, had induced, went on to develop themselves with awful severity through the winter. For a long time, there was a death and a funeral every two days. At one period there were only *six or seven* left well enough to attend to the sick, and to bury the dead. The graves were dug in the frozen ground, under a bluff near the sea; and whenever an interment was made, all traces of it were carefully obliterated upon the surface, for fear of the Indians. In the course of the winter, out of the whole number of one hundred, nearly *fifty* died. Of the *men,* only twenty survived; and these in a very emaciated and enfeebled condition.

The sickness was equally severe among the crew on board the *Mayflower,* which still remained in the harbor, it having been found not practicable for her to get ready to sail, on her return, before the winter had set in, and she was thus detained until spring. About half of her crew died from scurvy, consumptions, and fevers, while she lay at anchor in the bay.

RELATIONS WITH THE INDIANS

Thus far the relations of the colony with the Indians were certainly not of a promising character. What little intercourse had yet taken place had been hostile rather than friendly in its character. The colonists had entered the houses of the Indians, and had opened their graves, and taken property away—intending, it is true, to make compensation if an opportunity should occur. The Indians had, on one occasion, openly attacked the whites, and attempted to destroy them, and in several instances they had stolen their tools, and committed other depredations. Every indication denoted that they looked upon the newcomers with great distrust and suspicion, if they were not cherishing against them an avowed and decided hostility. But an occurrence took place, about the middle of March, which led to the establishment of an entirely different state of feeling, and relieved the colonists, for a long time to come, of all serious anxiety in respect to one of the most terrible of the dangers which had threatened them. The event marks, in some sense, the end of the dark and gloomy night of unbroken misfortune and calamity through which the colonists had been passing, and seemed to usher in a dawn of brighter and happier days. This auspicious occurrence was the visit of an Indian, named Samoset, taken in connection with results of great importance which flowed from it.

The Visit of Samoset

The occurrence referred to took place on a pleasant day, about the middle of March. The sun came out bright and warm that day, and everything betokened the return of spring. The leading members of the company were assembled together at the door of the common house, discussing some of their arrangements for the spring, when suddenly, much to their surprise, they saw an Indian coming boldly toward them, walking with a very self-possessed and confident air, along the little street between the log houses. He wore no clothing, except a simple garment, formed of the skin of a wild beast, about his loins. The lower edge of the garment was bordered by a species of fringe, about six inches long. His hair was black and straight, and hung loose down his back. He advanced boldly up to the men, saying something that sounded like "Welcome! welcome!"

As soon as the men recovered a little from their surprise, they began to ask questions of the newcomer, and he succeeded, partly by signs and gestures, and partly by broken English, in giving them a great deal of useful information about the country, and the inhabitants of it. He made them understand that the district, where they were, had been depopulated by a pestilence a few years before, and that was the reason that they had found the lands vacant, and the fields untilled. The other districts along the coast, and in the interior, were inhabited by different tribes. He gave the names of these tribes, and of the chiefs that ruled over them; and he represented the geographical situation of their several territories by a rude map, which he drew upon the ground. The chieftain, whose tribe occupied the country nearest them, he said, was Massasoit. His own name was Samoset. He had learned what he knew of the English language, he said, from the crews of vessels on the coast.

SAMOSET A GUEST FOR THE NIGHT

The people were, of course, greatly interested in receiving this intelligence. They continued their conference with their visitor for a long time, and, as a cool wind began to rise, during the interview, they brought a cloak and put it over him, at which he seemed much pleased. After a time, they gave him a good dinner, consisting of various articles of food, which were all doubtless great dainties to him. At any rate, he ate and drank what they offered him with great apparent satisfaction. At length, when night came on, they began to wish to have him go away, but he expressed a desire to stay all night. They were at first unwilling that he should remain, for fear of some treachery; but, as he seemed very desirous of it, they finally consented. They made up a bed for him in one of the houses, but they took the precaution to set a secret watch over him, in order to guard against any surprise.

He remained, however, quietly in his bed till morning, and then, after receiving his breakfast, he went away, promising to come again, and to bring some others with him.

VISIT OF MASSASOIT

Samoset kept his promise, for the next day he came again, accompanied by several other natives, and, what is more remarkable, they brought with them the tools which had been taken, some days before, from the place where they had been left in the woods.

Among other Indians that came with Samoset, was a certain one named Squanto, who had been, some years before, taken captive and carried to England, where he had remained for some time and had learned to speak the English language pretty well. He had, finally, about two years before this time, been brought back to his native land, and now happened, very providentially, to be in this region, so as to be brought by Samoset to serve as an interpreter. Samoset also reported that Massasoit himself was near at hand, accompanied by sixty of his tribe, and that he was desirous of opening friendly negotiations with the English, and of making a treaty of peace with them.

Massasoit accordingly soon came, and the negotiations were opened. We have not space to relate, in full, all the particulars of this curious interview, but can only briefly state, that Massasoit, attended by his brother, Quadequina, and all his men, halted on the top of a hill, and invited the English to come over to them; that the colonists hesitated to do this, but invited the Indians to come to them, which, however, they were not willing to do; that the colonists finally dispatched Squanto to learn what they wanted, and received answer on his return that they wanted someone sent over to parley with them, and that at length, one of their number, Mr. Winslow, bravely volunteered to go, carrying with him a pair of knives, and a copper chain with a trinket at the end of it, for a present. Mr. Winslow was kindly received, but was retained as a hostage, while the king, with a train of twenty men—leaving, however, their bows and arrows behind them—came down to the brook at the foot of the hill, and were met there by Miles Standish and seven others, who were sent forward to receive them; and, finally, the king was conducted with much ceremony to one of the log houses, and placed upon a seat of honor improvised for the occasion out of a green rug and three or four cushions—and many salutations and other marks of official respect were rendered to him, and then negotiations were formally opened, and the terms of a treaty of peace and friendship were discussed and agreed upon.

THE TREATY

The treaty thus made was a transaction of the utmost importance to the welfare and prosperity of the colony. It continued in force for more than fifty years, and was, on the whole, well and faithfully observed. The stipulations were, of course, very simple, both in substance and form. The articles were five in number, and were in substance as follows:—

1. That none of the Indians should molest or injure the colonists in any way, and if any did so, they should be given up to the colonists to be punished.

2. If any tools, or other property, belonging to the colonists, were taken by any of the Indians, the king should immediately cause them to be restored. And if any of the colonists should do any injury, or cause any damage to the Indians, ample reparation should be made.

3. The colonists were to assist Massasoit in any just war in which he should be engaged. And in case any other tribe should attack the colonists, Massasoit was to assist in defending them.

4. Massasoit was to send to all the other chieftains that occupied the surrounding country, informing them of the treaty he had made, and inviting them to come in and enter into similar engagements with the colony.

5. In all cases when Indians came to visit the colonists at their settlement, they should leave their bows and arrows behind; and the colonists should do the same, in respect to their guns, when they went to visit the Indians.

THE PROSPECTS BRIGHTEN

The foundation being thus laid for peaceful and friendly intercourse with the Indians, the little colony was relieved of what had been a very great source of anxiety to them. As the spring came on, too, the health of the company improved, and the men who were able to work commenced preparing the ground in their gardens for putting in seed, and also spaded up a number of acres of land, to plant in corn, barley, and peas. The Indians aided them a great deal in these works.

The sickness subsided, too, on board the *Mayflower;* and, early in April, the vessel set sail for England. She was to return again in the course of the summer, or another vessel was to come in her stead, with an additional number of emigrants, and with fresh supplies.

In a word, the members of the colony began to feel quite encouraged in respect to their prospects as the warm weather came on, and not one of them wished to return to England in the *Mayflower.*

EXCURSIONS DURING THE SUMMER

During the summer, although the greater portion of the colony remained at home, cultivating their fields and gardens, detachments were sent off from time to time; sometimes on foot, into the interior, to visit and traffic with the Indians; and sometimes in the shallop, along the coast, to explore the islands, bays, and harbors, and to enter into the mouths of the rivers. One of these expeditions entered and explored what is now Boston Harbor. They noted and examined the numerous islands in the bay. They sailed a little way up the Charles River, and they landed and made many observations on the main. They were so much pleased with the appearance of the country here, as to express regret that they had not discovered it before, and made their settlement there, but it was too late now to make the change.

THE FORTUNE

The summer, in a word, passed away pleasantly and prosperously; and, late in the fall, the hearts of the whole company were all gladdened by the arrival of a vessel from England, with news from their native land; and, also, with a reinforcement. The name of the vessel was the *Fortune;* and she brought thirty additional emigrants. This was a small number, but it is surprising that even so many had the courage to come, considering the extremely disheartening accounts which the *Mayflower* carried home.

Although the arrival of the *Fortune* thus furnished the colony with a reinforcement of men, still, she brought no provisions; and, as the winter was now setting in, and there would be no possibility of producing any more food until the next season, the condition of the settlement was rather worse than better, for a time, in consequence of there being more mouths to feed. These difficulties continued, indeed, for several years, and periods of great scarcity repeatedly occurred, which reduced the settlers sometimes to a state of great suffering. There was also very serious alarm about certain tribes of Indians, who were reported, on several occasions, to be preparing to make war on the colony. These rumors, however, proved unfounded. In the times of scarcity, also, which occurred, there seemed to be always some interposition of Providence to preserve them from actual destruction. Once they were saved by a fishing vessel which arrived off the coast, and from which they obtained a supply of sea-biscuit, which just carried them through to the next harvest of corn, and saved them from starving.

THE INDIAN POPULATION

The dangers which the new settlement had to fear from the savages were greatly diminished by the fact that the native population was at that time quite small; vast numbers of the Indians having been carried off by a pestilence which had ravaged the country a few years before. Some of the historians of the time considered this sickness as a special judgment from Heaven, sent upon the Indians on account of their cruelty to certain prisoners, which they took from the crew of a French vessel that came upon the coast, somewhere in Massachusetts Bay, a few years before, to trade for beaver skins. In consequence of some wrong or injury perpetrated upon them by the Frenchmen, the Indians attacked them, killed many of them, seized and burned their ship, and secured five of them as prisoners. These prisoners they distributed among the sachems in that part of the country, who kept them as slaves, employing them generally in the performance of menial work, and sometimes teasing and tormenting them for amusement.

"One of these men," the old account goes on to state, "out livinge the rest, had learned so much of their language as to rebuke them for their bloudy deede, saying, that God would be angry with them for it, and that hee would in his displeasure destroy them, but the Savages, boasting of their strength, replyed and sayd that they were so many that God could not kill them.

"But contrarywise in short time after, the hand of God fell heavily upon them, with such a mortall stroke that they died on heapes, as they lay in their houses; and the livinge that were able to shift for themselves would runne away and let them dy, and let their carkases ly above the ground without burial. For in a place where many inhabited there hath been but one left alive, to tell what became of the rest. The livinge not being able to bury the dead, they were left for

Crowes, Kites, and vermin to pray upon. And the bones and skulls upon the severall places of their habitations made such a spectacle after my comming into those parts, that as I travailed in that Forrest, nere the Massachusetts, it seemed to me a new found Golgotha."

It was in consequence of the sweeping away of so large a portion of the native population, a short time before the English colonists arrived, that they found so much cleared land abandoned and vacant, and ready for them to plant at once with wheat and corn; and also that the warlike power of the natives was so greatly reduced, that the colonists were generally able to defend themselves very easily against their hostility.

BAD MEN AMONG THE COLONISTS

Strange as it may seem, one of the chief sources of trouble in the colony arose from the influence of certain rude and unprincipled men among their number. Some incidents, illustrating the character and conduct of these men, will be related hereafter. These men were not members of the Leyden church, but adventurers, who had contrived to join themselves to the enterprise, and had come out in the *Mayflower*. Others, still, of similar character, came out in the vessels that arrived subsequently. These men sometimes made a great deal of trouble. Perhaps the difficulty was increased by the vigorous measures adopted by the colonists to control them. The stern spirit of the Puritan leaders was not likely to bend to anything like a conciliatory policy, in dealing with such men.

THE COLONY ESTABLISHED

Notwithstanding these difficulties and reverses, the colony went on increasing in numbers and stability every year. After a while, new settlements began to be established at different points about Massachusetts Bay. The old arrangement which had been made with the stockholders was terminated, and a new system adopted, which made every man the proprietor of his own house and land, and rendered each one dependent on the avails of his own labor alone. The population was increased by fresh arrivals. Many marriages took place, and births began to be quite frequent. In a word, the colony, in a few years, began to find that it was really taking root, and rapidly assuming the condition of a well-organized and self-sustaining community.

CHAPTER VI
MASSASOIT AND THE INDIANS

LIFE IN THE NEW SETTLEMENTS

During the few years that followed the first establishment of the Plymouth colony, and while the settlements were gradually becoming extended over the surrounding country, a great many singular events and extraordinary incidents occurred, which strikingly illustrate the mode of life which prevailed among the settlers, and the difficulties which they had to encounter. Perhaps the most curious and remarkable of these incidents arose out of the relations of the colonists with the Indians—and particularly with Massasoit, who was the grand sachem that ruled over most of the country that lay back of Plymouth, in the interior.

THE INDIANS SOMEWHAT TOO FRIENDLY

For some time after the treaty was made with Massasoit, as related in the last chapter, the colonists experienced some inconvenience from the visits of parties of Indians, who came rather too often to the settlement, for the sake apparently of the food which they obtained. The colonists, being very desirous of cultivating friendly relations with their new neighbors, especially since the treaty of peace and friendship which they had made with them, felt bound to entertain them hospitably when they came, but very soon they found that these visits became so frequent that they not only interfered with the work that was going on, but also threatened to encroach seriously on the stock of provisions.

SUSPICIONS AND FEARS

Besides this, the colonists often felt very uneasy during these visits, fearing some treachery. The artifice of the Indians, and their skill in devising stratagems of every kind, were very great, so that the English felt it necessary to be always on their guard. In later periods of the history of the colony the maneuvers and stratagems which were practiced by each side against the other were quite numerous, and many of them were of a very curious character.

THE WOODEN EFFIGIES

On one occasion, for example, a number of men journeying through the country, met with a large company of Indians, just before they were to encamp for the night. The Indians professed to be very friendly, and, after an exchange of civilities, both parties went on their way. The leader of the whites, however, saw something in the demeanor of the Indians, which led him to think they secretly entertained hostile intentions, and he expressed the opinion to his men that they would, in all probability, be attacked that night at their encampment.

In order to guard against this danger the leader resorted to the following ruse. As soon as the men had made their fire, and had constructed the little hut by the side of it, such as is usually made in such cases to shelter the sleepers from the night air, they cut a number of logs of wood, rolled them up in cloaks and blankets, to represent men, arranged them side by side in the hut before the fire, in the attitude of men sleeping. They then stationed themselves in a thicket nearby to watch the result.

About midnight they heard an Indian stealing cautiously up to the spot, to reconnoiter. He soon went away, but presently returned with a number of others, all armed with guns; for this was at a time when the use of firearms had extended considerably among the natives. The white men remained motionless, until the Indians, having crept stealthily up, took aim together, and fired, and then rushed on, with hideous yells, to finish the murderous work, which they supposed they had so well begun. The whites, however, now rushed suddenly out, and poured in a volley of bullets upon them. As their own guns were discharged they were, in a great measure, defenseless, and were, besides, so utterly confounded by this sudden change in the state of the case, that they seemed completely paralyzed. Every one of them was killed.

The stratagem.

Examples of this wily mode of warfare are innumerable in the history of the early settlements; and the artful character of the Indians, and the deceitful and treacherous practices to which they were accustomed, in making war, were very well known to the colonists at Plymouth, so that it is not surprising that they very much inclined to distrust any professions of friendship which such savages might make, and to discourage any tendency to too great a familiarity of intercourse. With these views, they regarded the frequent visits of large numbers of Indians at the settlement as a very serious evil.

An Embassage Sent to Massasoit

In June, 1621, a few months after the treaty of peace and friendship was made with Massasoit, it was concluded to send an embassage to that chieftain, in order, partly, to remedy this evil, and also, at the same time, to obtain information in respect to the condition of his country, and of his people, and to make some additional stipulations with him. Stephen Hopkins and Edward Winslow were the persons appointed to transact this business. They were to take with them Squanto, for an interpreter, and also some presents for Massasoit. The chief present was a horseman's coat, made of red cotton, and trimmed with gold lace. They also took a copper chain with them, suitable to be worn about the neck. The particular purpose of this chain will appear in the instructions.

The Instructions

The embassadors, if such they may be called, were to proceed to Massasoit's residence, and there deliver him, in substance, the following message from the governor of the colony. They were to say that the messengers were sent, and the presents which they bore were tendered, on the part of the colonists, as tokens of the love and goodwill which they felt for Massasoit, and for all his people. They were to say, moreover, that, situated as they were, it would not be in their power, thereafter, to entertain them as freely as they had done, and as they still would be glad to do, if circumstances permitted. Still, if the king himself came, he would always be very welcome, and if he wished to send any special friend, they would give him a cordial welcome, for the king's sake. And, in order that they might be sure that the visitor, in such a case, really came from the king, they sent the copper chain for a token; and requested that the king would always give it to any person whom he might send to visit the colony, so that, seeing the chain, they might know that the messenger was duly commissioned by his majesty, and treat him and his message with proper respect.

There were some other points to be attended to by the messengers; such as making arrangements for remunerating the owners, if they could be found, for the corn which the colonists had taken from the mounds at Cape Cod, and for obtaining a supply of seed corn for the next spring; and also for purchasing beaver skins, when any of the tribe had any to sell. With these instructions, and with Squanto for a guide, the messengers set forth on their mission.

An Indian Village

They went on for about fifteen miles into the interior, in a westerly direction, towards the place where the town of Taunton is now situated, and then came to the first of Massasoit's villages. Here they found a great number of men, women, and children, whom they recognized as having been among the visitors that had been so troublesome. It must be confessed, however, that these people did their best to acknowledge the hospitalities of the colonists, now that the visit was returned; for they gave the messengers a very cordial reception, and feasted them on the best they had; which consisted of a kind of corn cakes, the spawn of shad, and boiled musty acorns.

The Indians took occasion, now that the English were there with their guns, to ask them to shoot a crow for them, which happened to be in sight, complaining, at the same time, of the damage which the crows did to their corn. The men complied with this request, and shot the crow. The whole village were astonished to see at what distance the gun would kill.

Interview with Massasoit

The messengers continued their journey, and traveled nearly twenty-five miles that day. They passed other villages, and met several Indians by the way, who treated them in a very friendly manner, and aided them on their journey by all the means in their power. They passed a great many deserted fields, showing the decrease of population which had been caused by the plague. When night came on they encamped in the margin of a wood, where they slept in the open air.

The next morning they went on some miles further, and, at length, arrived at Massasoit's residence. The king was not at home, but his people immediately sent for him; and, when he arrived, he received the messengers in a very cordial manner. He conducted them into his wigwam, and there they produced their presents. The king clothed himself at once in his red coat, and put the copper chain about his neck; and then walked about, with an appearance of great pride and satisfaction, among his people, who, on their part, flocked around him, and gazed upon him with wonder and admiration.

Entertainment of the Embassadors

The embassadors delivered their message; and, in reply to it, the king made a set speech, in a very formal, and, as it would appear from the applause with which his people received it, in a very eloquent manner. The main thing was, that he fully assented to the wishes of the colonists, and renewed his promises of peace and friendship.

Night was now coming on, and the embassadors expected supper; but the king did not offer them any. The truth was, he had nothing. He was away on a hunting excursion, it seems, when he was called home to receive his visitors. The men were accordingly compelled to depend upon their own resources for food. But, to make amends, as it were, for this apparent want of hospitality in respect to the supper, the king assigned to his visitors places in his own royal bed for the night. This bed was a sort of platform, raised about a foot from the ground, and covered only with a mat. The platform was made large enough, according to the Indian usage, to accommodate not only the master of the house and his wife, but, also, all his visitors and friends. So, while the king and his squaw lay down at one end, the two messengers took their places at the other. Before they went to sleep, however, two other persons—chieftains that had come to see what was going on—came, and crowded themselves into the vacant space; so that the embassadors passed a very uncomfortable night. Their rest at night, in the royal bed, tired them more, they said, than all their fatiguing journeyings by day.

The Return of the Embassage

The next morning a number of the neighboring sachems came in to see the embassadors; and various conversations and ceremonies took place which cannot be here particularly described. There were also games, and feats of strength, and shooting at a mark, and other performances, which continued through the day. In the course of the day, the royal host contrived to furnish his guests with one meal, which, however, consisted only of fish. The men were by this time well-nigh exhausted by fatigue, and by want of proper food and rest. The king urged them to remain longer; but they found two nights in the king's bed as much as they could endure, and so they set off on the morning of the third day, as soon as it was daylight, on their return journey.

They suffered a great deal on the way, from hunger and exposure; and had it not been for the kindness and aid which they received from Indians who accompanied and followed them across the country, they would have been reduced to extreme distress. They were obliged to spend one night in camp, on the journey home; and, during the night, there came up a series of tremendous thunder showers, which put out their fires, and wet them through. The showers continued all the next day. They, however, journeyed on through the mud and rain, and, at night, reached home, weary, wayworn, footsore, hungry, and almost in a perishing state. They had, however successfully accomplished the object of their mission.

LOST BOY

Not long after this visit to Massasoit an expedition was sent to the southward, along the coast, to endeavor to recover a boy who had wandered away in that direction, and got lost. The name of the boy was John Billington. He was a bad boy, and belonged to a bad family. How it happened that such a family could gain admission to the company of the Puritans it is difficult to imagine.

THE BILLINGTON FAMILY

The Billington family did not belong to the original company of Puritans at Leyden, but joined the expedition in England. The head of the family was a rough and turbulent man, and he had two sons, John and Francis, who seemed to have resembled their father in character. They evinced a spirit of disaffection and insubordination during the voyage; and it was, in a great measure, on their account, and on that of some others like them, that the compact of civil government was drawn up and signed by all the colonists before leaving the ship, as related in a former chapter.

YOUNG JOHN BILLINGTON'S GUNPOWDER AFFAIR

While the colonists were all on board the *Mayflower* at Cape Cod, waiting for the selection of a site for the town, young John Billington one day came near blowing up the ship, and the whole company on board, with gunpowder. His father had opened a keg of gunpowder in one of the small cabins; and, after taking out what he wanted to use, he left the keg open in the cabin, with the remaining gunpowder in it. While he was absent on shore, most of the other men being also away, John took possession of this powder, and began to make squibs and fireworks with it, which he actually fired off in the cabin. At last he fired off a fowling-piece belonging to his father, which was there loaded, and the discharge set fire to the loose powder which was scattered about the floor. The noise of the report, of course, gave the alarm, and the people came rushing to the cabin. Very fortunately nothing except the scattered grains of powder took fire; but the whole company on board were very much alarmed, and everybody was indignant at such an inexcusable act of recklessness and folly.

JOHN BILLINGTON LOST

It was this John Billington that strayed away one day, and wandered off to the southward, along the coast, putting the colonists to a great deal of trouble to recover him. The party that was sent to seek him went in a boat. They took with them their old friend Squanto, for an interpreter, and also another Indian. They directed their course first to Barnstable Harbor[1]—though the place was then called by the Indian name of Cummaquid having had some reason to hope that they might there learn some tidings of the lost boy.

THE BEREAVED MOTHER AT CUMMAQUID

The party arrived at the mouth of the harbor in the night, but they found their way in and anchored the boat. In the morning they saw some Indians on the shore fishing for lobsters. The Indians invited them to land; and they did so, after taking proper precautions to guard against any treachery. The Indians, however, proved to be really friendly. They entertained the English hospitably at their camp, and brought their sachem, or chief, to see them, who told them that the boy was safe, and was at a place called Nauset, a little further along the coast; and that he, and two or three of his men, would go with them to show them the way there.

Before they set off, however, they received a visit from a very aged woman, not less—as they judged, than a hundred years old—who was very earnest to come and see them, having never had an opportunity to see any of the English. Instead, however, of appearing to be amused and gratified at the sight of the strangers, the spectacle seemed suddenly to overwhelm her with grief, so that she filled the air with her cries and lamentations.

The explanation was, that this poor woman was the mother of two of the Indians who had been carried off some years before, and sold as slaves, as related in a former chapter. They were her only sons

[1]See map on page 47.

who had thus been taken from her; and, being now entirely alone and helpless in her old age, the sight of the fellow countrymen of those who had thus wronged her brought on a paroxysm of distress and anguish which was wholly uncontrollable.

The colonists did and said all they could to comfort her. They told her that the men who had committed that crime were very bad men, and that the deed was as much execrated in England as it could be among her own people; "and that neither they, nor any of the people at Plymouth, would be guilty of such an outrage, not if they could gain all the skins in the country by it." They gave her, also, some presents, and, at last, left her somewhat appeased and comforted.

There are many persons who seem to think that an Indian or an African mother does not feel being bereaved of her children, like women of the Caucasian race. But incidents like these, which are innumerable in the history of these people, show that their natural affections are very strong.

PARLEY AT NAUSET

The party felt it necessary to proceed with great caution in approaching Nauset, for the Indians here were strange to them; and they were, moreover, beyond the limits of Massasoit's dominions. Besides, this was near the place where the exploring party which came from the *Mayflower,* along the coast, in the shallop, had been surprised and attacked by a party of Indians, as related in a former chapter. So, when they approached the shore, they all remained in the boat, and sent Squanto, with one of the other Indians, to the land, to communicate with Aspinet, the sachem of Nauset, and inform him for what purpose they had come; and to request him, in case he had the boy in his possession, to bring him to them on board the boat.

In a short time the messengers returned, bringing with them a great number of Indians, who waded out from the beach to where the boat was lying, grounded in the sand. The English would only allow two of these visitors to come on board, for fear of some treachery. They, however, held friendly intercourse with them as they stood around the boat, up to their knees in the water; and succeeded in trading with them for skins to some extent. It happened, curiously enough, that the very man whose corn they had taken from the mound was among this company; and the party settled his claim for remuneration very amicably, by promising him ample repayment if he would come to Plymouth, or, as he called it, to Patuxet. Or, if he desired it, they would send the compensation to him at any place that he might appoint.

THE LOST BOY RESTORED

The shallop lay thus, in the center of a group of savages standing around it in the water, nearly all day; though the persons were changed, for fresh parties were continually arriving, and others going away. Towards night the sachem came himself, attended by a hundred followers, and bringing the lost boy with him. Half of these men, who were armed with bows and arrows, remained on the shore. The others, who were unarmed, came off with the sachem to the boat; one of them bringing John Billington on his shoulders, not only safe and sound, but adorned with strings of beads, and other ornaments, which the Indians had bestowed upon him.

The party in the boat, on receiving the boy, made suitable presents to those who brought him, and especially to the one that John told them had first found him, and taken care of him. Then, after exchanging expressions of friendship and goodwill, the two companies took leave of each other, and the party in the boat set out on their return.

THE BILLINGTON SEA

The Billington family, which in other respects caused the little colony so much trouble, was the means of performing one service, which has resulted in perpetuating the name in connection with the geography of Massachusetts. This service was rendered by Francis Billington, the youngest son. He was rambling about near the place of the settlement, only a week or two after the landing; and, after ascending a high hill, he climbed up into a tall tree on the summit of it, to see what he could discover from the top. He espied among the trees, at a considerable distance inland, the glimmering, here and there, of what seemed to be a large sheet of water; and the next day he went with one of the seamen of the *Mayflower* to see what it was. It proved to be a large lake of fresh water; and the finding of it was quite a discovery, as it was well stocked with fish. It was called Fresh Lake for a long time; but, at length, in the next generation, it was named Billington Sea, in honor of the discoverer; and this was the only honor, it would seem, to which any of the family ever attained. As for the father of the family, his character grew worse and worse, until, at length, he came to the gallows for murder.

FRIENDLY RELATIONS WITH MASSASOIT

In the course of two or three years after the treaty was made with Massasoit, a great many other transactions took place with the different sachems in the country lying round about the settlement; and a great many different expeditions were sent forth, for a variety of purposes, which, however, cannot be here detailed. In all these negotiations and transactions the colonists remained faithful friends to Massasoit. They aided his friends and opposed his enemies; and, on every occasion when he needed their assistance, they rendered him all the aid in their power.

NEWS OF MASSASOIT'S SICKNESS

At length, about three years after the first establishment of the colony, news came to the settlement that Massasoit was sick, and was almost certain to die. It was at once determined to send a second embassage to him, to see if anything could be done to relieve him in his sickness. Mr. Winslow, the same who had been foremost in the mission sent before, was appointed for this second service. He was accompanied by an Englishman named John Hamden, who had come out to visit the colony, and whom some have supposed to be the great John Hampden, so celebrated in English history. They were to take with them an Indian named Hobbamock, for guide and interpreter.

DANGEROUS CHARACTER OF THIS MISSION

This mission was considered to be a very dangerous one; for the sachem who would be most likely to succeed Massasoit—a subordinate chieftain, named Conbatant—was not a friend to the colonists. Indeed, he had not been a friend to Massasoit, and the colonists had taken a decided part against him in some of his difficulties with his superior, and there was reason to fear that he was cherishing a secret resentment against the English, on this account; and, if so, he would be almost certain to wreak his vengeance on these messengers, if he should get them into his power, when away from their friends. It was possible that Massasoit might be dead, and that the whole government might have devolved upon Conbatant; so that the messengers, by entering the territory, would put themselves into his power; and, at any rate, they would be under the necessity of passing through his own particular territory on their way to Massasoit's residence.

But Winslow was a man who was never deterred by considerations of personal danger from rendering any service to the colony which might be required, and he was very ready to undertake the mission. John Hamden evinced an equal degree of courage and resolution. So, taking with them some simple medicines, and certain cordials, suitable for the sick, they set forth on their journey.

THE JOURNEY

They lodged the first night with some friendly Indians, on the way, and the next day they went on until they arrived within a few miles of Conbatant's village. Here, wishing, if possible, to obtain some intelligence, they stopped, and fired a gun, in order to attract the attention of any Indians that might chance to be in the neighborhood. Very soon several Indians appeared in view, coming out of the woods, in answer to the signal. They told the messengers that Massasoit was dead, and that he had been buried that day. On hearing this Hobbamock was greatly alarmed, and insisted that they must all immediately return. But Winslow and Hamden were not to be persuaded to abandon the enterprise so readily. After well considering the circumstances in which they were placed, they concluded that if Massasoit was really dead, and if Conbatant was going to succeed him, it was all the more important that they should go on and make a visit to the latter, and endeavor, if possible, to establish friendly relations with him at the commencement of his reign.

VISIT TO CONBATANT'S WIGWAM

So they went on about three miles further, which brought them to Conbatant's village. The sachem himself was not at home; but his wife received the messengers in a very friendly manner. She told them that she believed that Massasoit was dead; but she did not know certainly. So they sent forward a messenger to Massasoit's village, to ascertain the fact. They urged him to go and come back as soon as he possibly could, as there was no time to be lost.

The messenger returned about sunset, and reported that Massasoit was still living, but that he was at the point of death; and that there was no hope that the English, if they went on, would find him alive when they arrived.

ARRIVAL AT MASSASOIT'S

The two commissioners, however, immediately set out, and though they pressed onward as fast as they could go, it was late at night before they arrived at the end of their journey. When they came in sight of Massasoit's wigwam they found the dwelling itself, and the approaches to it, crowded with men and women, who were filling the air with the most unearthly shrieks and yells that ever were heard. These were the incantations and charms with which they were endeavoring to drive away the distemper under which the patient was suffering. The visitors forced their way in through this crowd, and when they reached the bedside they found the king lying helpless and insensible, his mouth so choked up that he could scarcely get breath, while a crowd of six or eight women were at work rubbing his arms and legs, in order to keep warmth in them.

The Sachem's Reception of His Visitors

As soon as some degree of silence was restored, the king, though he could not see, seemed to understand that somebody had come to visit him, and wished to know who it was. They told him it was *Winsnow,* which was the nearest that they could come to the right pronunciation of Mr. Winslow's name. The king then put out his hand, and Mr. Winslow took it in his own. The king then asked, or rather tried to ask, for he could scarcely make any intelligible sound, *"Keen Winsnow?"* which means, Is this Winslow? They told him that it really was. "Oh! Winsnow," said he, "I shall never see thy face again!"

Mr. Winslow Delivers His Message

Mr. Winslow then called Hobbamock forward, and, through him as an interpreter, he delivered the king the message which he brought from the governor of the colony. He said the governor had heard of his sickness, and was extremely sorry for it. He would have come himself to visit him if his public duties would have allowed. But he had sent two messengers to visit him, and to see if they could do anything for him; and had also sent some medicines for him, if he was willing to take them.

Mr. Winslow's Medical Practice

The king was very ready to take what had been brought for him; and Mr. Winslow immediately commenced his treatment. He first cleaned the poor patient's mouth, which, of itself, was a great relief to him. He then gave him some kind of cordial, which revived him still more; and finally administered some simple medicines. The condition of the patient was so much changed by these remedies that very soon his sight was restored, and he could speak a great deal better. He passed a very comfortable night; and, the next morning, he said that if he could only have a little broth, such as they gave him at Plymouth, when he visited the settlement, he thought it would do him a great deal of good; and he expressed a wish that Mr. Winslow would take his gun, and go and shoot a bird of some kind, and make him some broth. Although Mr. Winslow had no knowledge or experience in cooking, he was still very ready to try the experiment; but, before he was ready to go out after the bird, the king said he could not wait for that, but wished to have some broth made of such things as were already at hand. Mr. Winslow then went to work to prepare, in an earthen pipkin which they brought to him, a sort of concoction—half porridge, half broth—made out of bruised corn, and green leaves of different kinds of plants, which he gathered in the woods nearby, with some sassafras root for seasoning.

The king liked the broth very much; and he improved so rapidly after this, that when the next day two chickens arrived, which Mr. Winslow had sent back for to Plymouth, in order to make suitable broth for his patient, the king felt himself so well that he would not have the chickens killed at all, but would keep them for breeding.

Mr. Winslow's Practice Is Extended

The success which Mr. Winslow thus met with in treating the case of the king produced, of course, a great excitement throughout all the village, and a great number of sick people were brought to him to be cured. He did the best he could for these poor patients; and then, soon afterward, he set out with his companions on his return to Plymouth, with a feeling of great satisfaction, in having so successfully accomplished the object of his mission.

Peace and Prosperity of the Colony

It was, in a great measure, due to the treaty of friendship and alliance between the colony and Massasoit, which was so faithfully observed, on both sides, for so long a period, that the settlers were enabled to go on for many years in enlarging and extending their settlements, with so little molestation from the tribes of savages around them. When we consider how insignificant the numbers of the settlers were for the first four or five years after the establishment of the colony, and how completely they were environed by these pagan hordes, it seems to be by a wonderful interposition of Divine

Providence, that the heart of the chief leader of such savages was inclined, for so long a time, to look upon the strangers with favor; and to receive so cordially, and reciprocate so faithfully, the acts of kindness which they tendered to him in the spirit of peace and goodwill.

CHAPTER VII
MASSACHUSETTS BAY

The Case of Boston

The town of Plymouth was thus, as shown in the preceding chapters, the first established settlement of Europeans in New England. It was not, however, many years before a far more considerable and important center of immigration and colonization was established at some distance to the northward of it, in the vicinity of Boston. A group of settlements was here formed, which very rapidly increased in population and wealth, and soon became a most important center of influence and power, in respect to the whole country. These settlements constituted what was called the colony of Massachusetts Bay. Boston soon became the center and seat of government of the colony, though it was by no means the first place chosen by the colonists, as a site for a town. Gloucester, Salem, Charlestown, and Dorchester, all took precedence of it.

Fishing Villages

The first establishments that were made on the land bordering upon Boston Harbor, may be said to have been little more than fishing villages. Various expeditions were sent over from England, during the five or six years subsequent to the final establishment of the Plymouth Colony. These expeditions were sent out under the auspices of different companies in England, formed for the purpose, and their object, so far as respects the means of gaining a livelihood for those concerned in them, was mainly to trade with the Indians, and aid in fishing operations on the coast, by providing supplies of food for the fishermen, and also furnishing the means of curing the fish which should be taken, by means of stages erected on the shore, where the fish could be spread out in the sun to dry.

Religious Motives

While they depended on these pursuits mainly as a means of gaining a livelihood, a very large proportion of the emigrants were still greatly influenced by religious considerations in leaving their native land. King James the First had died, and King Charles I had succeeded him, but the nonconformists and separatists felt the pressure of the government upon them as heavily as ever, and all the expeditions which were formed to come to this country were recruited, almost entirely, from among the class in England that were objects of persecution there, on account of what their enemies called their puritanical fanaticism, though they themselves considered it simply their desire to worship God according to the dictates of their own conscience.

Salem

The word Salem means peace, and the existence of that name, as the designation of one of the most important towns in New England, is a memorial of one of the peculiar difficulties which the early settlers had to encounter. It will be recollected, that the whole American territory was originally considered as belonging to the crown. The crown granted it, on certain conditions, to two great companies—the Virginia and the Plymouth Company—the northern part, or New England, falling to the Plymouth Company. This Plymouth Company granted portions of the territory, from time to time, to different parties, and these grants were subject to so many changes, through acts of purchase, and sale, and lease, and sub-lease, and release, and other modes of transferring, that no little confusion resulted in the end, and sometimes it was a difficult question to decide which of two sets of claimants were entitled to a given territory—especially when, as it often happened, there was the title of possession, and occupancy on one side, and legal documentary right on the other.

Such a question arose in the case of a settlement made on the little river, Naumkeag. A man, who afterward became greatly distinguished in the annals of Massachusetts, John Endicott, came to the place to take possession of it, under a grant from the legal owners in England. He found, on his arrival, that a settlement had already been made there by a party that had at first established themselves farther to the eastward, on Cape Ann, but not having found that place eligible, and having suffered much hardship there, had now removed to Naumkeag, and had built huts, and made other improvements there. Of course, there arose at once that perpetually recurring question, in every new country, of the practical fact of occupancy and improvement against the theoretical right of government and law—a question often found very difficult to be decided.

The two parties, at the little settlement on the Naumkeag, did not, however, avail themselves of this excellent opportunity for a quarrel. They settled the question by an amicable arrangement, made Endicott their leader, and named their town Salem, in token of their determination that they would all live together in peace.

THE MASSACHUSETTS BAY COMPANY

The different colonies and settlements which had been established up to this time, were conducted by voluntary associations of men, of a commercial rather than of a governmental nature. They held grants, it is true, from the king and his government, but these were grants of territory, not of political power. They had, strictly speaking, no powers of government except such as they could establish among themselves by common consent. But we come now, in the year 1629, that is, seven years after the landing of the Pilgrims at Plymouth, to a transaction, which marks an era in the political history of the country, and that is, to a *formal grant of governmental power* by the king of England to a company, organized for promoting settlements in America. The company, to whom these new powers were granted, was called the Company of Massachusetts Bay. It was formed, after many negotiations which cannot be here particularly detailed, by the union of various parties, in England, who were interested in the different settlements already commenced, and who held various grants of territory. These parties, thus united, petitioned the king to bestow upon them, in a formal and legal manner, authority to establish a regular government for their colonies, and the king did so.

The Patent

The document, by which these powers were granted, was called a *patent*. It was drawn up in great form, engrossed in the usual style of such documents, upon parchment, and authenticated by the royal signature, and by the ponderous seals of state that were affixed to it. An exact copy of this charter is contained in the records of that day. It is written in a very quaint and technical style, and in antique characters and abbreviations, and with many formalities and phrases, some in Latin—and is so full in its details, that a transcription of it would occupy more than twenty pages of this book. All that is necessary here is to say, in general terms, that it authorized the company in England to organize a complete government for the colonies that should be settled within the limits of their territory—which was the territory bordering on Massachusetts Bay. They could make laws, elect the governor and all necessary magistrates, declare and carry on war, when necessary, against all enemies, and transport to America any of the subjects of the king who might desire to go, except such as he should forbid by name.

They could also choose their own associates and successors, and the powers thus conferred were to be held by them and the associates and successors thus chosen, forever.

New Impulse Given to Colonization

The company, after being invested with these new and greatly increased powers, engaged with new energy in making arrangements for enlarging and extending the colonies under their charge. They organized themselves under their new charter, and held frequent meetings, in which they devised and prepared to carry into effect very important measures. The records of these meetings still remain, and it is curious to read the minute account which they give of all the business which came before the council; such as the various applications which were made to them from parties intending to emigrate, lists of articles to be sent out, rules and regulations made, and disagreements and difficulties discussed and settled. Within a very short time after the patent was granted them, they fitted out an expedition of six vessels, containing a large store of supplies and a very considerable number of emigrants. Among these last were three hundred men, eighty women and girls, and twenty-six children. There were also a hundred and forty head of cattle and forty goats. There were several ministers sent out, too, in this company.

BEGINNING OF RELIGIOUS DISSENSION

Thus far a large majority of the settlers in New England had belonged to the class of Puritans and separatists from the established church of England—but not all. There were many persons that had been induced to join them in their emigration who were not of their faith, and many who belonged to the company in England, too, or who were interested in various ways in the expeditions which were sent out, and still adhered to the Episcopal mode of worship. Two of these, John and Thomas Browne, being dissatisfied with the congregational worship established in the colony, determined, soon after their arrival, to set up a separate worship for themselves and those who agreed with them, which was to be conducted according to the liturgy of the Church of England—the very system which the colonists had crossed the wide ocean to escape from, considering it, as they did, as a corruption of the word of God. The colonists were much displeased at this movement, and after some angry discussion on the subject, in which the two Brownes evinced a resolute and inflexible determination to adhere to their design, the governor, John Endicott, told them that New England was no place for such as they, and so he ordered them to be put on board a return ship, and sent them directly back to England.

They appealed to the company in England, and a good deal of debate and discussion followed on the question of the right of the colonists to expel from the country those who differed from them in religious opinion.

ARGUMENT IN FAVOR OF THE COLONISTS

The argument in favor of the right of the colonists to do this was, that the very object for which they had left their native land, and crossed the wide ocean to seek a new home in the wilderness, was to escape from a religion of rites and ceremonies; and after having done and suffered so much to place themselves entirely beyond the influences of such a system, those who upheld it had no right to follow them and renew the trouble, by attempting to introduce among them again the germs of an evil which had already been the means of causing them so much suffering.

THE ARGUMENT AGAINST THE COLONISTS

On the other hand, it was replied that the grand principle which the colonists had put forward as the life and soul of their undertaking, in attempting to found new settlements in America, was religious liberty—the right of every man to worship God according to his own conscience. The whole ground of their complaint against the government of their native land was that they were not allowed to judge for themselves in respect to questions of Christian faith and practice; and now they were denying that right to their fellow settlers in America. The circumstances being changed, they were now attempting to enforce religious uniformity, under their own government, by the same kind of persecution which they had complained of so bitterly when it had been employed as a means of suppressing their dissent under the government of their native land.

THE RESULT

This question came up in various forms a great many times during the early history of the colonies, and though for a time the settlers insisted upon their right to exclude from their territory such as were opposed to them in their religious faith and practice, and in many instances exercised this power, in the end this doctrine was abandoned, and it has long been an established principle in America that civil government should be separated entirely from all questions of religious faith and practice, and that all men, whatever may be their principles of belief or unbelief, and whatever may be the ecclesiastical organizations to which they belong, should enjoy absolutely the same civil rights and privileges, and stand in all respects under a perfectly equal footing in the presence of government and law. In no other country in the world, however, is this principle yet admitted, while still in all countries it is gradually but surely gaining ground.

TRANSFER OF THE CHARTER AND GOVERNMENT TO AMERICA

When the government of King Charles granted the patent to the Massachusetts Bay Company, authorizing them to make laws and establish a government for their colonies in America, it was the understanding, on both sides, that the seat of government should be in London, at the offices of the company; just as the government of India was managed for many years by the East India Company, from executive and legislative halls contained in a vast edifice called the East India House, in Leadenhall Street, London. But there was nothing in the patent itself which confined the company to London; and, within a year or two after the grant was made, the question arose whether it would not be better to transfer the whole charter, government and all, across the water, to the territory covered by it.

There were many reasons for doing this which cannot be here fully detailed. There were, however, great doubts whether the grantees had, legally, power to do it. They finally concluded that they possessed the power; and that it would be best for all concerned that it should be exercised. They accordingly, at once, made arrangements for carrying this plan into effect.

At a meeting of the company, held for this purpose, in London, the officers—who, as it happened, were persons so situated that it was not convenient for them to remove to America—resigned, and a new set were appointed, consisting of persons who were willing to emigrate. These men were very carefully selected, after much examination and inquiry. The leading man among them, the one who was elected governor, and on whom, of course, the chief responsibility connected with this grand movement rested, was John Winthrop.

JOHN WINTHROP

John Winthrop was an English gentleman of wealth and high position, and also of great energy of character. He was admirably qualified to fulfill well the arduous duties that he was called upon to perform; and he subsequently held a very prominent place, and, for a long time, wielded a very extended and powerful influence over all the affairs of the colony. He at once made arrangements for equipping and sending out a large number of vessels with stores and additional emigrants. There were no less than seventeen of these vessels that sailed in the course of the summer; and they carried a thousand men. The first portion of the fleet, which Governor Winthrop led personally, consisted of eleven vessels, although only four of them were ready to sail on the same day. The whole, however, in addition to the great number of men and women, took out a vast supply of tools, and utensils, and materials, and stores of all kinds. There were also carried in the vessels two hundred and forty cows, and sixty horses.

The name of the vessel in which Winthrop himself sailed was the *Arbella*. She was named from a lady—the Lady Arbella Johnson—who was the wife of one of the most wealthy and influential members of the company, and who, with her husband, were passengers on this voyage. She was a titled lady according to the usages of the English aristocracy, being the daughter of an earl; and had been accustomed, all her life, to the refinements and splendor enjoyed by the English nobility. But she sacrificed all, from her love to her husband and her interest in the enterprise in which he was engaged.

The little fleet sailed from the Isle of Wight in March, 1630. The governor kept a minute journal of all that happened on the voyage. This journal is filled with very interesting incidents and details, which bring the scenes of the voyage almost as distinctly before our minds as if we had actually been eyewitnesses to them.

ARTICLES OF CONSORTSHIP

There were four ships, in all, ready to sail at the same time. These four came down from Southampton to Cowes, on the north side of the Isle of Wight, intending to take their departure from that port.

The others had not yet completed their preparation, and so remained at Southampton.

The names of the four vessels ready were the *Arbella,* the *Ambrose,* the *Jewel,* and the *Talbot.* Before sailing, the masters of the four vessels held a conference, and drew up what they called articles of consortship, providing a set of rules which they were all to observe at sea, in order to keep together; or to facilitate their reassembling in case of getting separated. The different vessels were assigned their respective ranks. The commander of the *Arbella* was to be the admiral, that of another vessel the vice admiral, and of a third the rear admiral; and a system of signals was agreed upon, by which orders could be transmitted, and other communications effected at sea; and distinct provision was made for joint and concerted action under any and all the emergencies which might reasonably be expected to arise. Various other preparations, and arrangements of a similar character, were also made.

GOVERNOR WINTHROP'S FAMILY

Governor Winthrop left his wife in England, with the expectation that she would follow him to America subsequently. The state of her health did not allow of her crossing the Atlantic at this time. So he left her at their former home in Groton, in England, with some of the children. Two of his sons went with him. After leaving his wife he wrote to her almost every day until he sailed; and his letters breathe such a spirit of affectionate tenderness for her, and such sorrow at being obliged to separate from her, even for a time, as makes the correspondence a very touching one to all who read it. On the evening before he sailed from Cowes he wrote to her what he supposed would be his last letter. The following extract from it will give a good idea of Winthrop's character as a husband and father.

WINTHROP'S LETTER TO HIS WIFE

"My faithful and dear wife,
"It pleaseth God that thou shouldst once again hear from me before our departure, and I hope this shall come safe to

thy hands. I know it will be a great refreshing to thee. And blessed be his mercy that I can write thee so good news, that we are all in very good health, and having tried our ships' entertainment now more than a week, we find it agree very well with us. Our boys are well and cheerful, and have no mind of home. They lie with me, and sleep as soundly in a rug—for we use no sheets here—as ever they did at Groton; and so I do myself, I praise God."

Then, after giving some account of the different vessels, and of the arrangements made for the voyage, he closes his letter as follows:—

"And now, my sweet soul, I must take my last farewell of thee in Old England. It goeth very near to my heart to leave thee, but I know to whom I have committed thee, even to him who loves thee better than any husband can, who hath taken account of the hairs of thy head, and puts all thy tears in his bottle, who can, and if it be for his glory, will bring us together again with peace and comfort."

And so he went on, endeavoring to comfort and encourage her, saying that she must not fear anything which might befall him, since even if they did not meet on earth they were sure to meet in heaven; for the sea, he said, could not drown him, nor any enemies destroy him, in such a manner as to deprive her of her husband—and promising to think of her and pray with her in spirit every Monday and Friday, at five o'clock in the evening, as they had agreed—and adding finally, "I will only take thee now and my sweet children in mine arms, and kiss and embrace you all, and so leave you with my God. Farewell! Farewell! I bless you all in the name of the Lord Jesus."

His Son Left Behind

The oldest of "the boys," as he called them in his letter, who set out to make the voyage with their father, was, unfortunately, left behind at Cowes. His name was Henry. He was despatched to the shore by his father, together with some other persons, in order to send off an ox and some sheep that were to be put on board. They sent off the cattle, but did not come themselves; and the little fleet, being obliged to sail that night, put to sea without them—Governor Winthrop hoping to take his son up at Yarmouth, where they were to touch. It afterward appeared that Henry and the others had attempted to come off in the evening, but a heavy gale of wind was blowing, and the tide being against them, they could not reach the vessel. They all afterwards took passage in other ships, and thus Henry, in the end, rejoined his father. But he did not live long. He was, unfortunately, drowned, a day or two after his arrival, in a little creek near Salem. He was quite a young man, and had just been married before he left England. His young wife remained behind, with her mother, when he sailed for America. She was inconsolable on receiving the news of her husband's death.

PASSING THE NEEDLES

The fleet sailed at length, and passing down the Solent, which is the narrow channel of water lying between the Isle of Wight and the mainland, came to the Needles—which are several immense cliffs of chalk, standing out detached from the shore, at the western extremity of the island. They are remains of what was once a portion of the land, which is here formed of a range of chalk hills of vast elevation. These Needles, enormous in magnitude as they are, with sides perfectly precipitous, and the sea roaring and raging incessantly among them at the base, form a magnificent spectacle, which, in storms, becomes terribly sublime. When the fleet passed the spot, there was a Dutch East Indiaman, of a thousand tons burden, lying a wreck among these rocks. They could see men on board attempting, apparently, to save some of the property. The vessel herself lay so high out of the water, where she had been driven by the waves, that there was obviously no possibility of ever getting her afloat again.

THE DUNKIRKERS

The fleet came to anchor in the port of Yarmouth, and remained there some days, in order that the vessels might take in their last supplies of wood and water, and fresh provisions; and also to receive some passengers that had been delayed. Some of the passengers, too, among whom the Lady Arbella is particularly mentioned, went on shore "to refresh themselves."

At length all was ready, and the fleet weighed anchor and put to sea, not, however, without considerable anxiety on the part of the ships' companies—for there was a report at Yarmouth that there was a fleet of ten Spanish war vessels, from Dunkirk, lying in the channel to intercept them—Spain being at that time at war with England, and Dunkirk being one of her principal naval ports. They, however, were not intimidated by this rumor, but sailed on down the channel, and soon were out of sight of land. Presently, there came into view a number of vessels in the offing, which the commanders of the vessels at once supposed were the Dunkirkers. They immediately began to prepare for a battle.

They took down the cabin partitions, so as to make room to work the guns, threw overboard all the straw from the beds, and everything specially in danger of being set on fire during the combat, armed all the men, and assigned them their quarters, and made arrangements for sending the Lady Arbella, and all the other women and children below, where they would be out of danger. Then they all assembled on the upper deck, and held a meeting for prayer, to implore the Divine protection in the danger which seemed to be impending over them.

The effect of the prayer was to calm and quiet the excitement in a remarkable manner. All seemed perfectly self-possessed and composed. There was not a woman or child that showed any fear. The captain, too, seemed so cool and collected as to impart great courage and confidence to his men.

It was now a little after noon. The fleet of supposed Dunkirkers was about three miles distant, and were slowly drawing nearer. The captain of the *Arbella*, who, according to the arrangement which had been made, acted as admiral of the fleet, wishing to show the enemy that he was not afraid of them, and also wishing that if there was to be any contest, it should take place before night came on, changed his course, and advanced in a direction to meet the strange vessels— making signals, at the same time, to the other three vessels of his fleet to follow. It was not long, however, before they found that the whole was a false alarm. The supposed Dunkirkers proved to be friendly French and English vessels, bound, some to the Mediterranean, and others to Canada and Newfoundland. So, instead of firing shot and shell at each other, they only exchanged friendly salutes, and "all our fear," as the governor says in his journal, "was turned into mirth and friendly entertainment."

RULES AND REGULATIONS

A set of rules and regulations for the government of the passengers, while on board the vessels, had been drawn up and posted conspicuously where all could read them—and these rules, which were very necessary for the peace and comfort of the several companies embarked, were strictly enforced. There were several young men on board the *Arbella,* and two of them, before the vessel had even left the channel, became in some way or other engaged in a quarrel which ended in a fight. This was a flagrant infraction of the rules, and the culprits were condemned to walk the deck all the rest of the day, with their hands tied behind them. Another young man, for contemptuous and mutinous words uttered to the governor, was put in irons, and kept in that condition until he acknowledged his fault, and promised to conduct himself better in time to come.

Another curious case of misdemeanor came to light, toward the end of the voyage. One of the men, a servant of one of the company, made a bargain with a child to give him a little box, in payment for which the child was to bring him three biscuits a day out of his allowance—that is, one biscuit at each meal. The box was not worth sixpence, but it pleased the child's fancy, and he agreed to the bargain—and he had been giving the man three biscuits every day, for ten days, before the thing was discovered. The man had sold the biscuits which he thus obtained to other persons on board. To punish him for this chicanery, he was sentenced to stand two hours, with his hands tied up to a bar fastened over his head in the rigging, and a basket full of heavy stones hanging about his neck.

Way of Curing Sick Children

The vessels encountered a great deal of cold and stormy weather on the voyage; and, at one time, after a heavy gale, the wind in the afternoon began to go down; but the children, and many of the maids who had the care of them, were very sick, and the children lay crying and groaning in the cabin, wet, cold, and miserable. Their parents resorted to a singular measure, though it proved very effectual, to remedy the difficulty. The plan which they adopted was this.

They stretched a rope from one mast to another, on the upper deck, and then, bringing up all the boys and girls, and several of the young women with them, they arranged them on the opposite sides of this rope, and set them to pulling against each other—the whole line being, of course, swayed this way and that, all the time, by the rolling motion of the vessel. In this way they all soon got into a great frolic, and were also thoroughly warmed by the exercise; so that after playing in this manner for half an hour they went below again, both "well and merry."

End of the Voyage

Varied by scenes and incidents like these, and many others wholly unlike them, but which cannot be here narrated, the voyage was continued, week after week, until, at length the vessels arrived in Massachusetts Bay. The company of emigrants landed, and took up their abode chiefly in Charlestown and Salem; though, soon afterward, a portion of the settlers removed to the peninsula of Shawmut, and there commenced the town of Boston. It is said, however, that one small house had been built there three or four years before.

The emigrants under Governor Winthrop found the condition of things in the colony very discouraging when they first arrived. The settlements were very scantily supplied with provisions; and much sickness prevailed. Great numbers died in the course of the fall and winter. The Lady Arbella died within a month after her arrival; and her husband, overwhelmed with grief at her death, which he felt that he himself had caused, very soon followed her to the grave.

THE NEW GOVERNMENT

Although the arrival of these vessels, and those which immediately followed them, bringing with them, as they did, the charter itself, and also a complete set of officers elected under it, transferred the organization of government from England to America, it did not, by any means, transfer it to the *inhabitants of the colony*. All legislative power was vested in a kind of board of directors, which was called the Court of Assistants; but, in choosing these assistants, no one had a vote excepting actual *members of the company;* and none were members of the company without both owning a share in the stock, and also being voted in by the other members. Thus the government of all the settlements on the shores of Massachusetts Bay was vested in what is called a close corporation, though the seat of the corporation had been now transferred from England to America, the colony itself remaining entirely under its control, as before.

This state of things was not likely long to endure. It soon became necessary, or began to be necessary, to admit the inhabitants to a share of the power which the charter conferred upon the company. This share, in process of time, became larger and larger, until, at length, as will hereafter appear, the whole government was transferred to the colonists themselves; and the republican system, substantially as existing at the present day, was fully inaugurated.

SPREAD OF THE SETTLEMENTS

In the meantime, as years rolled on, the population of the towns on the sea coast increased, and settlements began gradually to extend into the interior. One of the greatest checks to this extension was fear of the Indians. For, although the Indians were generally friendly, and many treaties of peace and amity were made from time to time with the different tribes, there were still frequent alarms, and often periods of open hostility. Many times the settlers were obliged to take their arms with them into the fields, in conducting their agricultural operations; and, not unfrequently, they brought their wives and children too, leaving the houses empty, for fear of some sudden attack upon them, in the absence of the men. Often two or more families would combine in making these arrangements, the men exchanging work, and their wives keeping each other company, for mutual aid and protection.[1]

The governments of the different colonies took every possible precaution to avoid giving the Indians just cause of offence; and they punished very severely any wrongs committed against them by individual settlers, so far as the authors of such wrongs could be discovered. But these efforts could not always be successful. The Indians would often commit acts of hostility under pretense of avenging real or imaginary injuries which they had received. Sometimes, even, the desire of a colony to live in peace with the natives, would cause them to make a treaty of amity with one tribe which, of itself, would prove an occasion of offence, and, perhaps, of open war, with another—rivals and enemies of the first. Thus, periods of anxiety and alarm, in respect to the Indians, were perpetually recurring; and much suffering was caused by them. Still the work of colonization and settlement went on, until at length, the whole line of the coast, and the courses of all the great rivers flowing from the interior, were dotted with rising villages and towns, the abodes of European and Christian intelligence and civilization.

---

[1] See p. ii.

CHAPTER VIII
THE DUTCH ON THE HUDSON

FIRST RUMORS OF THE DUTCH SETTLEMENT ON THE HUDSON

Seven or eight years after the settlement at Plymouth had become established, certain vague rumors came to the colonists there, from time to time, chiefly through the Indians, of a company of Dutch emigrants, who had established themselves at the mouth of the Hudson River, two or three hundred miles to the southward. The Plymouth men questioned the Indians very closely on the subject, but all the information which they could obtain was vague and unsatisfactory, until at length, in the spring of 1627, a letter came to Plymouth, written both in French and in Dutch, and dated from Fort Amsterdam, in Manhattan. It was addressed to the Governor of Plymouth Colony, and was signed Isaac de Razier.

THE CORRESPONDENCE

The correspondence commenced in an extremely friendly tone— the object of the first letter appearing to be chiefly to send an amicable greeting, on the part of the Dutch colony to the English one, and to express their desire to live on neighborly and friendly terms with them. At the same time, the letter contained a proposition to open a trade with the English colony; and there were also in it certain intimations in respect to the trade of the Indians in the region of Plymouth, which awakened some uneasiness in the minds of the Plymouth people.

Governor Bradford, for Bradford was at this time the governor of the Plymouth Colony, replied at length, reciprocating all the kind expressions in the letter from the Dutch settlers, and expressing a readiness to trade with them, in case any circumstances should arise to make an interchange of commodities advantageous on both sides. He, however, frankly added, that in respect to the Indians, the king, his sovereign, reserved the traffic exclusively for his own subjects, those, namely, who were settled at Plymouth, and in the other colonies on those coasts.

To this communication De Razier replied, in another letter, in which, though he still maintained a very polite and friendly tone, he yet denied that the English had any exclusive right to the trade with the Indians, and that their own government—that is, the government of Holland—would protect them in their rights, in case any of the members of the Dutch colony should wish to enter into this trade. Several other letters, written in the same spirit, were afterward interchanged—so that, on the whole, the correspondence did not end quite so agreeably as it had begun.

In this correspondence, the letters on the part of the Dutch, in the first instance at least, were written in duplicate, one copy in the Dutch, and another in the French language. Governor Bradford answered in Dutch as well as he could. He had learned to speak the language while he was in Holland, but he could not write it very well; and he apologized in his letter for his rude and imperfect mode of expressing himself, which he begged his correspondent to excuse.

VISIT OF DE RAZIER

Although the number of letters comprised in this correspondence was not great, still the difficulties and delays were such, in sending them, that the correspondence was protracted through the whole summer, and it ended, in the fall, by De Razier's making a voyage through Long Island Sound to Buzzard's Bay, and thence crossing over to Plymouth to visit the English colony. Governor Bradford sent guides to meet him at his ship, and to conduct him across the country—although most of the overland journey was performed by following the course of the rivers, in a boat, which the guides took with them for that purpose.

Condition of the Town of Plymouth at That Time

De Razier wrote home to the government of Holland a full account of this voyage, and of what he observed at Plymouth, and this letter was found, a few years since, in the royal archives at The Hague. Among other things, he gives a particular account of the town of Plymouth, as it then appeared. His account is substantially as follows.

"The town lies," he says, "on the slope of a hill, stretching eastward toward the sea coast, with a broad street, about eight hundred feet long, leading down the hill, and another street crossing it in the middle. The houses are constructed of hewn planks, with gardens, which are also enclosed behind and at the sides with hewn planks, so that these houses and courtyards are arranged in very good order, with a stockade, against a sudden attack; and at the ends of the streets are three wooden gates. In the center, on the cross street, stands the governor's house, before which is a square enclosure, upon which four guns are mounted, so as to command the streets.

"Upon the hill they have a large square house, with a flat roof, made of thick sawn planks, supported by sapling beams, upon the top of which they have six cannons, which shoot iron balls of four and five pounds, and command the surrounding country.

"The lower part of this building they use for a church, where they preach on Sundays. They assemble, by beat of drum, each with his musket or firelock, in front of the captain's door. They have their cloaks on, and place themselves in order, three abreast, and are led by a sergeant, *without* beat of drum. Behind the sergeant comes the governor, in a long robe; beside him, on the right hand, comes the preacher, with his cloak on; and, on the left hand, the captain, with his side arms and cloak on, and with a small cane in his hand. And so they march in good order, and each sets his arms down near him. Thus they are constantly on their guard night and day."

Besides this graphic picture of the village, and of the ordinary life of the settlers, the report contains a very full account of the general condition of the colony at that time, and describes in detail the nature of the government, the character of the laws and usages in force, and the employments and resources of the inhabitants.

FORT AMSTERDAM

The Dutch settlement at Fort Amsterdam, from which De Razier came, had been established several years. It was, in fact, only three or four years after the landing at Plymouth that the first company of Dutch emigrants arrived at the mouth of the Hudson. They came very much against the will of the English, and especially of both the London and Plymouth companies. A company, similar to these, called the West India Company, had been organized in Holland, and it was under the auspices of this company that the first party of emigrants came out. When the London and Plymouth companies in England heard that such a plan was on foot, they addressed a strong remonstrance against it to the English government, and the English government made a communication to the Dutch government on the subject. But the Dutch government gave an evasive answer. They did not think that the West India Company were forming any such plan. They were sending out vessels, from time to time, to fish and trade upon the coast, but the government had no reason to believe that they intended a permanent settlement.

Accordingly, the West India Company went on with their operations uninterrupted. Perhaps they did not intend to make any permanent settlement, but only to build trading houses, here and there, for the convenience of trafficking with the Indians; and these trading houses, being necessarily made strong, and capable of being defended, soon took the character of forts. There were several of these stations established on the Hudson River, and on the shores adjacent to its mouth; but one, called Fort Amsterdam, which was built on Manhattan Island, the site of the city of New York, soon became the most important of them. In 1624, a number of Dutch families came out under the charge of a governor or director named Peter Minuit, and built a town around Fort Amsterdam. They named the town

New Amsterdam. This little town was situated on the lower point of the island, and the fort occupied a portion of the ground which is now known as the Battery. The town was built to the eastward of it, along the shore.

In about two years after they commenced the settlement, wishing to enlarge their territory, in some degree, and also to make themselves secure in their possession of it, they bought the whole island of Manhattan, from the Indians, for a sum equal to about twenty-four dollars. The island is thirteen miles long, and, upon an average, nearly two miles wide.

GREAT PRIZE CAPTURED

Holland was, at this period, one of the greatest naval powers in the world. Not only were the government in possession of a large number of first class men-of-war, but the commercial ships, owned by private persons, were extremely numerous; and, by means of them, the Dutch merchants carried on an immense traffic in every part of the world. It was natural, under these circumstance, that the Dutch West India Company should be well provided with ships, and should maintain a very frequent intercourse with their settlements. Many of these ships were armed, and some of them were commissioned by the government to act as cruisers.

Holland was at war with Spain at this time, and the Spaniards held very extensive possessions in the central part of South America, from which large quantities of silver were shipped every year. These silver laden ships were accustomed to sail in fleets, under convoy; the convoy being supposed to be strong enough to protect the whole squadron. But the Dutch West India Company assembled a number of their ships, and sent them out to the West Indies, under the command of an able admiral; and he contrived to intercept one of these fleets, and captured the whole of them. There was silver on board of them to the amount of five million dollars!

This silver was immediately taken to Holland; and, on dividing it, a very large portion was assigned to the shareholders of the company. Their dividends rose to 50 percent, and the whole country was greatly excited by this marvelous success. The effect was to bring the affairs of the company very prominently before the minds of the people, and greatly to stimulate emigration to their colony at New Amsterdam.

The Patroons

In order to increase still more rapidly the settlement of the country, and to induce a higher and more wealthy class of people to emigrate, arrangements were made by the company for granting very large tracts of land to persons of substance and condition, on certain terms. These persons were called patroons, and the grants made to them were intended to constitute them a species of nobility.

The terms were, in substance, that the patroon should found a colony to consist, within four years, of not less than fifty persons over fifteen years of age. He might choose any place for his colony that he liked, provided it was not within a certain number of miles of any settlement previously commenced by some other patroon; and each one was entitled to four miles of frontage on any river or seashore, and to go back as far into the interior as the wants of his settlers might require. Only he must extinguish the Indian title to the land which he should thus occupy, by paying the Indians whatever might be its fair value.

Over the colony thus established the patroon was to reign like a little prince, or, rather, like a feudal baron of the Middle Ages—subject, however, to the general control of the company. He was authorized to hunt, and fish, and trade, in all parts of the country; and to send his expeditions for this purpose to any part of the coast, from Florida to Newfoundland; only he was bound to bring all that he should obtain back to New Amsterdam, and pay a certain percentage of the value into the treasury of the company.

The patroons were, however, absolutely prohibited from manufacturing any kind of clothing, on pain of banishment. This was for the benefit of the cloth manufacturers in Holland.

Failure of the Plan

We cannot trace, in detail, the operation of this attempt to build up new settlements in the wilderness on the plan of the ancient feudal institutions of Europe. It is sufficient to say, that like all other attempts to lay the foundations of an aristocratic system in America, it was destined not to succeed. A great number of tracts of land were taken up under this arrangement, and a great many attempts made to establish colonies upon them. But germs of difficulty and contention soon began to spring up. The patroons quarreled with the directors of the company on the one side, and with their own tenants and servants on the other. These difficulties increased with the lapse of time, until, at length, the whole system was overborne and submerged by the advancing tide of republican principle and feeling; though it has left relics and landmarks of its existence among the institutions of New York, which remain to this day.

PROGRESS OF THE COLONY

In the meantime, however, the general colony, notwithstanding these difficulties, went on prosperously. The settlements were gradually extended up the rivers, and along the sea coasts adjacent to New Amsterdam. The English people, and particularly the London and Plymouth companies, watched the growth, and the rising importance, of these settlements with a very jealous eye; but they could not succeed in inducing the government to interfere. At length, however, accident gave them an opportunity of calling the attention of the government to the subject, in such a manner, as to force them to take some action in respect to it.

SEIZURE OF THE DUTCH GOVERNOR IN ENGLAND

In 1632, which was about eight years after the colony was founded, Minuit, the governor, concluded to make a visit to his native land; and, in company with some other persons of distinction in the colony, and with some families who desired to return, he embarked on board one of the company's ships. The party crossed the ocean in safety; but, in entering the English Channel, they encountered a storm which compelled them to put into Plymouth. As soon as the fact that this vessel had arrived in Plymouth Harbor, came to the knowledge of the Plymouth Company, they caused the ship to be seized, and commenced an action at law against her, on a charge of having traded to a country subject to the king of England. Governor Minuit went immediately to London, and complained to the Dutch minister there, and he at once laid the case before the king of England, and demanded that the ship should be released.

Then followed a long negotiation and discussion; in the course of which the whole history of the continent seems to have passed under review. The result of it was, that each party adhered to its own views in respect to the general question. The Dutch government insisted that the country was rightfully theirs, they having been the first to settle in it; and having, moreover, fairly purchased the territory of the Indians, who were the original proprietors. The English, on the other hand, maintained that their rights of discovery and occupation in America covered the whole extent of the coast, from Newfoundland to Florida; and these rights they could not surrender. Finally, however, for the sake of peace—as it would be, at the time, much against the interest of England to go to war with the Dutch— the English government concluded to give up the vessel; though they did it under protest, maintaining that justice was on their side, and reserving the right to enforce their claims to the possession of the territory, whenever they should judge it expedient for them to do so.

Of course, there could be no solid or permanent peace under this state of things. Just so soon as the objections, on the part of the English, to go to war with the Dutch should be removed, an attack on Fort Amsterdam was sure to be made.

COLLISIONS IN AMERICA

Besides the difficulties and discussions which thus took place between the two governments in Europe, collisions soon began to occur in America. One of the companies in England sent a vessel with a cargo of goods, under the charge of a resolute captain, to the Hudson River, with orders to sell them to the Indians there, in exchange for furs. When he arrived at the mouth of the river, the Dutch governor, who was at that time Wouter Van Twiller, sent word to him to demand what his business was in those waters. He said he was going up the river to trade with the Indians, and asked if the

American History Vol. IV

governor would allow him to go peaceably. The governor answered in the negative, and warned him off the coast. The captain replied that if he could not go with the governor's consent he should go without it, and he immediately went on past the fort and town, and sailed up the river. The governor sent a force up after him. They found him encamped on the bank of the river, and busily engaged in trafficking with the Indians. The Dutch landed, pulled down his tent, seized his goods, and put them on board his vessel, and compelled him to go down the river again, and put to sea.

Of course, when the report of these proceedings was conveyed to the company in England, it aroused them to the highest pitch of indignation and rage.

TROUBLE WITH THE INDIANS

In addition to the difficulties and disputes in which the colony became thus involved with their English neighbors, the settlers suffered very severely, in repeated instances, from wars with the Indians. The manner in which one of these wars originated illustrates, very strikingly, the condition of things existing at the day, between the emigrants and the natives.

It was the custom of the settlers to purchase of the Indians such articles as they could produce, or procure, and particularly furs and skins. The Indians would set their traps in the forests through which they ranged, and then bring the furs that they obtained to New Amsterdam, or to the nearest European settlement, for sale— taking in exchange blankets, ornaments, and, finally, muskets and gunpowder. This trade was extremely profitable to the settlers; for the furs were generally estimated at a very low price by the Indians, while in the European markets many of them were of great value.

THE WECKQUAESGECK INDIANS

Peter Minuit, who has already been spoken of as the first director or governor of the colony, had a farm on the island of Manhattan, where there lived some farm servants, who were employed to till the ground. There was a tribe of Indians, called the Weckquaesgeck

Indians, that inhabited the territory on the mainland contiguous to the island, where now is situated the town of Westchester. One of these Indians, accompanied by a small boy, his nephew, in coming from the Indian village to the island, with a quantity of furs which he had for sale, was waylaid by the governor's men, and robbed and murdered by them. The boy escaped. The men, of course, kept what they had done a close secret. The Indians complained of the outrage; but, either from want of evidence, or from some other cause, they could obtain no redress. The robbers, in due time, brought their stolen goods, cautiously, into the market, as if they had obtained them honestly; and the whole affair was gradually forgotten. It slept thus, in oblivion, for twenty years!

INDIAN MODE OF REDRESSING A WRONG

It seems that it was an established principle among the North American Indians at this time, that, whenever a murder was committed, it devolved upon the nearest relative of the murdered man to punish the crime by slaying the murderer; and, in any case in which the criminal belonged to another tribe, and was protected by them, and shielded from punishment, then the avenger of blood was bound to take the life of someone of the tribe—anyone whom he could most easily come at—to avenge the death of his relative. This was on the principle that the tribe or community to which the assassin belonged, by screening him from punishment, made themselves individually responsible for the crime.

This seems to us a very rude sort of justice, but it was the best which the nature of the case admitted. Indeed, something analogous to it continues in force in many civilized communities to the present day; as in those cases where a man has a claim against a town or other corporation which the corporation neglects to pay, and is empowered by the law to attach the property of any member of the corporation, to satisfy his claim, leaving the person whose property is thus taken to recover it again of the body of which he is a member. There is this essential difference, however, between the two cases, that the man whose property is taken to satisfy a public claim may be reimbursed again by those for whom he is held responsible; but the life of the innocent man taken in retaliation for a crime which another has committed, can never be restored.

The Indian Boy Performs His Duty

The Indian boy who made his escape when his uncle was murdered, felt that upon him rested the obligation, according to the law of the land, to punish the crime. He made a solemn vow, that so soon as he should arrive at manhood he would faithfully perform this duty. He remembered this vow for twenty years, and then he went deliberately at work to fulfill it.

He fixed upon a man named Claets Smits as his victim. Smits was a wheelwright by trade, and was somewhat advanced in life. He lived in a small house by himself, near a little creek or bay, at some distance from the town. The Indian went to the house with some furs, which he offered to exchange for blankets, and while Smits was leaning over the chest where he kept his blankets, selecting such as he was disposed to sell, the Indian struck him on the head with an axe, and killed him on the spot. He then, as the Dutch say, in giving their account of the transaction, plundered the house of all that he valued, and went away with his booty.

It is highly probable, in fact, that this story of the plunder is true, and if so, it shows that the Indian considered the law of retaliation, in its bearing upon himself; as conferring a right quite as much as enjoining a duty. The fact that a near relative of his had been robbed and murdered, gave him the power to rob and murder, to the same amount, with impunity. Indeed, it is highly probable that the Indian lawgivers, in ordaining this mode of avenging and punishing crime, relied on the pleasure which the avengers would experience, and the advantage and the glory which they would acquire, by the act of retaliation, as their main inducement to fidelity in executing the trust.

War

Governor Kieft, who was the chief magistrate at this time presiding over the colony, immediately sent to the Weckquaesgeck village, and demanded that the Indian who had slain Smits should be delivered up to him. The Indians replied that, in acting as he had done, he had only avenged a murder which had been committed many years before, and had remained unpunished to that day; that, in so doing, he had acted strictly in accordance with their law, and that he could not be given up. Both parties then began immediately to prepare for war.

Some little time elapsed before hostilities were commenced. The governor, who represented the Dutch West India Company rather than the people of the colony, was eager to proceed in the most prompt and efficient manner; but the colonists themselves, who knew from past experience what awful sufferings an Indian war would bring upon them, were very desirous to preserve peace. In the meantime, while the debates and negotiations were going on, new collisions took place, which increased the irritation—and, in the end, a war broke out, in which other tribes were gradually drawn in, and which, for a long period, filled the whole country with terror and distress. The scattered hamlets and solitary farms of the settlers were pillaged and burnt, women were violated and murdered, children carried into captivity, and innumerable lives destroyed. On the other hand, the civilized party, in this horrid contest, was not a whit behind the savage in the perpetration of atrocities. The villages of the Indians were burnt, their fields were devastated, men, women, and children were slaughtered, and the miserable people were hunted, like beasts of prey, in the most merciless manner.

The war lasted about two years, and the result of it upon the colony was nearly to depopulate it. All the outlying farms and settlements were utterly devastated. A great portion of the stock of cattle, which had been brought over from Holland at great expense, was destroyed. The people that remained, gathering together all the cattle that they could save, sought refuge in and around the fort—where now is the New York Battery—and, in order to protect the cattle, they built a very strong palisade across the island, from river to river, a little way back of the town. This palisade served the purpose of a wall—and the celebrated Wall Street of the present day marks the line on which it stood. Within the small space included between this line and the Battery, all that remained of the colony were crowded together, in a state of unspeakable anxiety and distress.

END OF THE WAR

It was the governor, Kieft, who was chiefly responsible for the extreme severity with which the war was carried on. The colonists themselves were inclined to much more moderate measures. There were other subjects of controversy, also, between them and the governor, and in the end they sent a memorial to the Company, demanding his recall. The Company, after a full examination of the question, ordered Kieft to return to Holland, and sent out a new governor in his place. In connection with this change of administration, peace was made with the Indians, and soon afterward the colony resumed its career of growth and prosperity.

The new governor, sent out by the West India Company on this occasion, was the celebrated Petrus Stuyvesant. He continued to preside over the colony for about twenty years, during which time it made great advances in population, wealth, and power. His administration, at the end of that time, was brought very suddenly to a close, by transactions which transferred the whole colony to the dominion of Great Britain.

The circumstances connected with this change will be related in the next chapter.

CHAPTER IX
THE CONQUEST OF NEW NETHERLAND

Duration of the Dutch Power

The Colony of New Netherland, for that was the name given to the whole district, occupied by the settlements of the Dutch West India Company, on the Hudson River and along the adjacent coasts, remained in the possession of the Dutch for about forty years. Then came the change alluded to at the close of the last chapter. The colony was taken possession of by an English force. The Dutch officials were expelled from power. The Dutch names, in respect to all the more important places, were abolished, and English names introduced in their stead; and the whole territory was brought under English rule. The circumstances under which this change was effected were as follows.

Rise of the Puritans to Power in England

During the period above referred to, as those of my readers, who are at all familiar with English history, will remember, two great revolutions took place in England. The first of these revolutions brought the English monarchy to an end for a time, and raised the Puritan and republican party to power. Then, after a few years, a counter-revolution took place—the Puritan party was deposed, and the monarchy restored.

It was during the reign of James I, and in the early part of that of Charles I, that the Puritans suffered that persecution on the part of the government, which induced so many of them to forsake their native land, and to attempt to found new settlements in America. Of course, only a small portion of those who agreed with the Pilgrims in principle, could accompany them in their exile. The great mass of the dissentients remained behind, and, notwithstanding all the efforts made by the government to suppress the party, their numbers and their power continually increased. Charles I, when he came to the throne, on the death of James, evinced no disposition to conciliate these men. He resorted to measures more and more stern and decided, in proportion as the power, and what he called the obstinacy, of the malcontents increased. Other questions, besides religious ones, arose, and in these, large classes of the English people took sides with the Puritans against the king. In a word, after a long struggle, the particulars of which cannot be related here, the Puritans and republicans gained the day. The king was brought to trial for his alleged crimes, was condemned, and publicly executed in front of his royal palace in London; and, for many years afterward, the government of the country was under the control of the party which had dethroned him—their great leader, Oliver Cromwell, ruling the empire under the title of Protector instead of that of King.

RESTORATION OF THE MONARCHY

But though the monarchical party was thus vanquished for a time, it was not destroyed. The royalists still adhered to their opinions, and held themselves in a state of readiness to rise at any time in favor of the restoration of the old state of things, the moment an opportunity should arrive. Their party gradually increased. Various difficulties were encountered by the republican government, and many causes of discontent among the people arose. Still everything went on tolerably well so long as Oliver Cromwell lived—but when at length he was no longer at the helm, the great royalist party of the kingdom rose, as it were, as one man, to reinstate the monarchy, and to place Charles II on the throne. The Puritans and republicans, now greatly diminished in numbers, and reduced in power, made no serious attempt to prevent them.

THE MONARCHY AND THE COLONIES

Of course, the inhabitants of the various colonies in America were well pleased with the revolution in England, which brought their friends and partisans into power—and when, at length, the monarchy was again restored, they naturally looked with some apprehension on the change. They had, indeed, some reason to be alarmed, for it was not long after the accession of Charles II to the throne, before the government began to turn their attention to American affairs. It is necessary, they began to say, that we should look a little into the condition of those young republics across the water, and to bring them under some wholesome regulations, and into some proper and permanent subjection to the crown, or their independence of spirit, and their insubordination, will make us trouble someday.

THE SOLICITUDE OF THE GOVERNMENT NOT WITHOUT CAUSE

There was, moreover, some cause for the suspicions which the king's government were disposed to entertain in regard to the loyalty of the colonies. The Massachusetts people did not proclaim the king until fifteen months after his restoration, and then the government made rules and regulations to prevent the manifestation of any great enthusiasm on the occasion. The legislature also appointed a committee to draw up an exposition of the rights of the colonial government, and the principles avowed in this exposition were such as to restrict the power of the king over them within very narrow limits. The Massachusetts colony, too, began to coin money, and this had always been considered as the special prerogative of the supreme power. The colony, also, had the presumption to send over commissioners, to lay their claims and pretensions, in respect to the management of their own affairs, before the king. All these things evinced a spirit of independence and of sturdy resolution, on the part of the colonists, not likely to be at all in harmony with the ideas of a monarch of the Stuart line.

In respect to the act of coining money, however, the colonial government escaped, as it proved, very easily. It so happened, that one of the devices on the coin was the representation of a tree of some sort. When called to account for this coining business, in the king's council chamber, the commissioners produced one of the coins, and showed the tree upon it to the king and to the councilors, representing it to them as denoting the Royal Oak, so called—that is, the oak in which King Charles had concealed himself, some years before, when pursued by the soldiers of Cromwell, which had thus been the means of saving his life. The king, who, with all the stern severity of his principles as a monarch, was, personally, one of the most light and trifling of men that ever lived, was delighted at seeing this tree. He said that the old Puritans in Boston were "jolly dogs," and waived all objection to the act of coining.

This figure of a tree upon the coin was not intended, it appears, to represent any royal oak at all, but was simply designed as an emblematic token of the forest wealth of the new world.

Measures Adopted by the Government

The measures which the government determined to adopt, in order to regain, and to establish on a permanent footing, what they considered the rightful authority of the king over his American possessions, were these:

First, to make a grant to the brother of the king, James, Duke of York, who subsequently succeeded to the throne under the title of James II, of all the territory both to the north and to the south of the existing New England colonies. These grants included, on the north, all the lands lying between the Kennebec and the St. Croix; and, on the southern side, all between the Connecticut and the Delaware. This last grant included, of course, the Dutch settlement of New Netherlands—the English government maintaining, as they always had done, that the Dutch had no rightful claim to that country, but that in making settlements there they had always been trespassers on English ground.

Secondly, to send out five commissioners, with a squadron of ships of war, and a small body of troops. The ostensible object of this force was to dispossess the Dutch, and so transfer the territory which they had occupied to the government of the Duke of York. But another part of their design, and, perhaps, the most important one in their view, was, that by such a demonstration of force they expected to overawe the colonists, and to invest the commissioners with power and authority to carry out more completely the intentions of the king.

The grant was accordingly made, and the commissioners were appointed. Colonel Nicoll, a military officer of distinction, and a member of the household of the Duke of York, was placed at the head of the commission, and made commander of the forces.

There were certain difficulties and disputes, too, that had sprung up between the different colonies, which the commissioners were instructed to inquire into and arrange. It was expected, that by taking advantage of these dissensions, the commissioners would be able to aid themselves very much in working their way to a position of influence and control in colonial affairs.

It was supposed, too, that the colonists would be so much interested in the great ostensible object of the expedition, namely, to conquer the Dutch territory, and bring it under English dominion, that they would be less ready to take alarm at the appearance of such a force among them. Indeed, the colonists were to be called upon to furnish their respective quotas of troops to accompany the ships to the Hudson; so that the light in which the expedition would chiefly present itself to them, at the outset, would be that of a friendly power asking for the alliance and cooperation of the colonists, for the accomplishment of an object of common interest to all concerned. In a word, the whole affair was very adroitly arranged.

SUSPICIONS AND FEARS OF THE BOSTONIANS

The suspicions and fears of the people of Boston were, nevertheless, not wholly allayed by these precautions. They called out their militia companies, and put everything in order for action, in case any action should be required. The legislature appointed two of the most trustworthy men to take the patent, that is, the parchment roll containing the grant of the governmental power to the Massachusetts Bay Company, made by Charles I, and to put it away in a sure and secret place, to prevent the possibility of its being seized. They also made rules and regulations in regard to the reception of the squadron, when it should arrive. By these rules the movements of the officers, and the landing of the troops, were much restricted, and were held entirely under the control of the colonial legislature.

In a word, while the colonists were willing to receive the expedition courteously, they would do it only in such way, and on such conditions, as that the supremacy of the colonial government, within the limits of the authority granted them by their patent, should be fully recognized and maintained.

ARRIVAL OF THE COMMISSIONERS

Of course it was impossible to foresee at what time a squadron crossing the Atlantic, by the force of wind alone—especially as there could be no decisive information in respect to the time of its sailing—might be expected to arrive. The suspense and uncertainty of the people of Boston were at length, however, suddenly terminated on Saturday afternoon, at the close of a pleasant summer's day, just as the sun was going down, and the people were beginning their preparations for the commencement of holy time—which, according to their custom, dated from sunset on Saturday evening—by seeing two English ships of war, both armed with formidable batteries of cannon, coming up the harbor. The spectacle produced great excitement. Indeed, the event marked quite an era in the history of the colony, since this was the first time that the harbor of Boston had been honored by the presence of any national ships. All the vessels that had before this time come into these waters had been the private ventures of individual merchants, or company ships, owned and controlled by councils and boards of directors. The arrival of national vessels, armed and equipped for war, with national troops on board of them, and an executive commission, clothed with great power, by direct authority from the king, was something certainly new; and the town of Boston, and all the surrounding settlements, were thrown into a state of great excitement.

ORDER OF PROCEDURE BY THE COMMISSIONERS

As has already been stated, the commissioners were clothed with extensive powers to inquire into all the affairs of the colony, and to regulate them in accordance with the views of the government at home. They did not, however, at first, introduce any topics of this kind, but adroitly confined themselves to the business likely to be agreeable to the colonists; that is, the proposed expedition to the mouth of the Hudson River, to dispossess the Dutch. They communicated this design to the governor of the colony, and asked of him to provide as many troops as he could spare to accompany the expedition.

The governor convened the legislature, and various negotiations and enactments ensued, the details of which cannot be here given. The result was, that the colony voted to raise two hundred men, and to furnish them with the necessary equipments and supplies. The Connecticut colony also aided in the same way; and two men, of high standing and character, were appointed by the respective governments, to join the commissioners in the expedition.

The News Reaches New Amsterdam

Thus far Stuyvesant and the government at New Amsterdam were wholly unaware of the danger which threatened them; but now, suddenly, they became greatly excited and alarmed, by receiving a full account of all these proceedings, through the captain of a vessel who came from some part of New England, and had obtained his information from Boston. This captain, whose name was Willett, told Governor Stuyvesant that the king of England had granted the whole of the Dutch territory to his brother, the Duke of York; that the duke had fitted out an expedition to come and take possession of it; that he had appointed Colonel Nicoll, one of the duke's followers, and an officer of great ability, to take command of the expedition; that the king had furnished a body of troops, and several ships of war; that the colonies in New England were to furnish additional troops; and that the appearance of the squadron in the harbor might be expected at any day.

Preparations for Defense

Of course this intelligence produced the greatest excitement and alarm in New Amsterdam. The burgomasters were called together, and vigorous measures were immediately adopted to prepare for defense. New works were commenced for fortifying the city. Stores of gunpowder were provided. Some vessels that were about sailing from the port, with provisions, were detained, in order to increase the reserve of supplies; and trustworthy persons were sent forward, along the shores of Long Island Sound, to watch for the first appearance of the ships, which were expected to approach in that direction. In a word, everything was done that could possibly aid in putting the place in good condition for defense, and to guard against surprise.

CUNNING MANEUVERING OF THE ENGLISH

Unfortunately, however, for them, just at this time dispatches arrived from Holland, giving an account of the sailing of Nicoll's expedition, and representing it in a totally different light from that in which the account which Willett had given placed it. It seems that the English government had succeeded in deceiving the Dutch government, in respect to the object of the expedition. In their representations to the Bostonians, they had held up the conquest of New Amsterdam as the great object in view, and had kept the designs of the government, in respect to the internal affairs of the colonies, almost entirely out of sight.

In their communications with the Dutch, on the other hand, they had represented the object of the commission to be merely the remodeling of the existing English colonies, and bringing them back to a wholesome subjection to the authority of the mother country, in respect to church and state. The Dutch were deceived by this cunning maneuver and the officers of the company in Holland wrote, accordingly, to Governor Stuyvesant, and assured him, in order to allay any unnecessary anxiety which he might otherwise feel, that if he should hear of the arrival of an English squadron on the American coast, he need give himself no uneasiness on account of it, as the only object that the government had in view in sending it, was to regulate the internal affairs of their own colonies, and not at all to molest their neighbors.

FALSE SECURITY

In consequence of receiving these dispatches, Governor Stuyvesant was at once convinced that Capt. Willett had been misinformed, or else that he willfully made false statements, to accomplish some sinister purpose. By this time Willett, it appears, had come into the harbor again. He was brought before the governor, and closely cross-examined. He was frightened; and concluded, that since he had brought himself into such difficulty by telling the truth, the best thing that he could now do would be to say what it would be most agreeable for his auditors to hear. So he explained that there had been a general belief in Boston that Colonel Nicoll's destination was New Amsterdam, but he had since learned, that if any such design had been entertained it was now abandoned. The troops had been disembarked at Boston, and the frigates discharged; and the commissioners were devoting themselves wholly to the work of settling the disputes, and defining the boundaries of the different colonies in New England, without the least idea of coming to capture New Amsterdam, or to molest it in any way.

Accordingly the work on the fortifications was stopped, the vessels that had been detained put to sea, with their cargoes, the watchmen which had had been sent out were called home, and Governor Stuyvesant, having some business up the river, at Fort Orange, went away out of town, leaving everything, as he imagined, in security.

ARRIVAL OF THE SQUADRON

In the meantime the squadron had been going on completing its preparations in Boston harbor, and, in due time, had sailed for the Hudson; and, in two or three weeks from the time that Stuyvesant left the city, an express messenger came to him to summon him back to the capital, with the intelligence that the enemy were certainly coming. Just twenty-four hours after his arrival he saw, with anguish and alarm, the first ship of the squadron sailing up the harbor.

FEELING OF THE PEOPLE OF THE COLONY

The loss of the two or three weeks which had elapsed was, of course, irreparable, but the governor immediately commenced a most vigorous course of action, with the view of doing all that it was now possible to do to avert the impending danger. His interest, however, it must be observed, was, in many respects, different from that of the people of the colony. He was not *their* magistrate, but rather that of the great company of merchants in Holland, who held and governed the colony—the people themselves having very little actual participation in the direction of public affairs. Now it was of immense importance to the West India Company in Holland that they should retain their hold upon their colony, but it was of comparatively little consequence to the settlers—since they were not allowed to govern themselves—whether they had one set of masters over them or another.

Indeed, the mode of government established in all the English colonies, and the character of the institutions that prevailed among them, were such as to throw a very large share of the political power into the hands of the people; so that the settlers on the Hudson had good reason to regard the transfer of the territory to English rule as being rather of the nature of an act of emancipation for them, than one of conquest and captivity.

Besides this, a very considerable portion of the people were English. The Dutch had been the first to open the settlement, but great numbers of English families had afterward come in, so that, sometimes, it was found necessary that the public documents should be issued in both languages, in order to ensure their proper promulgation to the whole people.

Thus, while the governor was in a fever of apprehension and excitement at the approach of the English force, the people were disposed to take the matter very coolly; and they were not at all disposed to hazard the destruction of the town, or to submit to any other very extraordinary sacrifices, to avert the impending revolution.

RESOLUTE CONDUCT OF THE GOVERNOR

Still the power was, for the present, in the governor's hands, and he determined to exercise it to the utmost to defend the trust which had been committed to him. He caused a draft to be made of one-third of all the men within his jurisdiction, and required them to appear with spade, pickaxe, or wheelbarrow, to work upon the fortifications. He caused the gates of the city to be shut, and closely guarded. He brought more cannon, and mounted them on the fort. He forbade the removal of any grain from the town, and ordered all the brewers to stop their operations of malt-making. He sent orders up the river to the different military posts, and also to those on the shores of Long Island, and on the mainland, requiring all the men who could be spared from the garrisons to be sent down. The soldiers that he had under his command were armed and equipped, and required to hold themselves prepared to fall into their ranks at a moment's notice, and the guns on the fort were allotted, and trained to the embrasures, ready for action.

The response of the people to all this ardor and energy on the part of the governor was very feeble. The settlers upon the outlying farms sent word in, that they had their wives and families to protect, and could not come to help defend the town. The commanders of the forts, up the river, replied to the governor's call for all the men that they could spare, by saying that they were in such imminent danger of attacks from the Indians, that they could not spare any. The consequence was, that when the governor came to muster his troops, and estimate his resources, it proved that the sum total of the means at his command, for defending—what afterward became the vast commercial capital of half the world—consisted of twenty-two pieces of cannon on the earthworks of the fort, and a company of from ninety to a hundred men.

PROCEEDINGS OF COLONEL NICOLL

In the meantime, the advance ships of the squadron lay in the bay, waiting for the arrival of the others. During this interval, however, Colonel Nicoll was not idle. He established a strict blockade of the river. He took possession of a blockhouse, or small fort, on Staten Island. He stopped all intercommunication over the waters of the bay and harbor, between the different farms and settlements on the shores, and, in enforcing this non-intercourse, he captured one or two boats laden with cattle, which one of the colonists was conveying to his farm. He issued a proclamation, too, addressed to the farmers in all that region, forbidding them to carry provisions of any kind into the town, promising, at the same time, to all who should submit peaceably to the authority of the king of England, that they should not be molested, but should be protected in life and property, and threatening them, on the other hand, with fire and sword, if they attempted to make any resistance.

The farmers seem to have been rather pleased than otherwise, at receiving such a warning, as it furnished them with a good excuse for not rendering the governor the cooperation which he demanded. So they remained quietly at their homes, and took no part in the contest.

A PARLEY

As soon as the governor had completed the measures of preparation which required the most prompt and immediate attention, he sent a deputation, consisting of four prominent personages—a councilor, a burgomaster, and two clergymen—with a letter to the commander of the fleet, to demand for what purpose, and by what authority, they had come into the harbor with such a force. They delivered the letter, and were promised an answer the next morning. Accordingly, the next morning, Colonel Nicoll, in his turn, sent a deputation, consisting of the same number of persons— all officers of rank under his command. This deputation conveyed to the governor a formal demand for the surrender of the town, and of all the forts in the vicinity, and the whole territory which they commanded, to his majesty the King of England, to whom, as the summons alleged, they rightfully belonged. The summons was accompanied by a proclamation, declaring that in case the surrender was made, all who should peaceably submit to it, should be protected, both in their persons and property.

Reception of the Summons

The governor was greatly excited, and much perplexed, on receiving this summons, especially on account of the effect which he feared the proclamation which accompanied it would have upon the people. He determined not to make it known to them. He summoned a meeting of the burgomasters, that is the city magistrates, and informed them of the demand which had been made, and called upon them to adopt and carry into effect still more vigorous measures for defense. The council of burgomasters asked him for a copy of the communication which he had received from the English, but he refused to furnish one.

Great Excitement in the Town

The intelligence that the governor had received a summons to deliver up the city, but that he would not divulge the terms and conditions that were offered, spread through the town, and produced great excitement among the citizens. It was on Saturday that the summons had come and the meeting of the council was held, and the excitement throughout the town having continued and increased during Sunday, on Monday morning a meeting of some of the principal citizens was called, and resolutions were passed insisting on the governor's producing the communication which he had received, that the people might know exactly what the English demanded. When this action of the citizens was communicated to the governor, he went in person to the meeting, and endeavored to persuade the members of it to recede from the ground they had taken. To produce such a document, which belonged wholly to the administrative department of government, at the call of the populace, would be, he said, entirely contrary to all military usage and propriety; and, it would certainly cause him to be censured by the authorities at home. Besides, the influence of it would be to distract the minds of the people, introduce divisions among them, and discourage them in their defense of the town.

But the meeting would not relinquish its demand, and the governor, finally, though in a state of great excitement, and sorely against his will, produced the document.

A New Communication

The trouble did not end here. The next day an officer from Colonel Nicoll came under a flag of truce, to the town, and held an interview with the governor outside the walls. When the governor returned into the town he had a paper in his hands, which the officer had given him, and which was supposed to contain some new proposals in respect to a surrender, and, perhaps, to offer still more favorable terms—as, in fact, it did. The governor went into the Stadt House, where the council of burgomasters were assembled, with the paper in his hand. They wished to know what it contained. The governor admitted that it was a fresh communication from the commander of the fleet, but that the contents of the paper were for himself alone. He should act according to his own discretion in respect to the use which he should make of it.

In fact, the governor was getting out of patience with the pressure which was exerted upon him; and, finally, when he found that the burgomasters were firm, and insisted upon knowing precisely how the case stood in respect to the demand of the enemy, he fell into a passion, tore the paper in pieces, and went off in a rage to his quarters in the fort.

Excitement among the People

As soon as the knowledge of this occurrence spread among the people the excitement passed all bounds. The men who were at work upon the fortifications threw down their tools, and gathered in crowds in the streets, and before the doors of the Stadt House. They uttered curses, loud and deep, against the governor, and against the company whose agent and minister he was. The company, they declared, had always oppressed and misgoverned the colony. They would rather be under the English government than to have things continue as they had been. Besides, it was useless to attempt to defend the town against the English force. It was impossible to suppose that, with his hundred men and twenty-two guns, the governor could resist the power of so many heavily armed men of war, and the four or five hundred troops which were on board, ready at any moment to land. It was better to yield at once, and spare the useless effusion of blood.

Not content with these clamors, the meeting sent a committee of three to the fort, to demand of the governor a copy of the letter. The governor, finding that an actual insurrection of the town against his authority was imminent, and harassed and exasperated beyond measure, ordered the pieces of the letter to be put together again, and a copy made out, which copy he sent to the burgomasters, and they communicated it to the people.

It contained an assurance, on the part of Colonel Nicoll, that in case of a transfer of the colony to the English government, the Dutch settlers should all continue to enjoy the same privileges, in respect to going and coming, as heretofore; that if any of them should wish to return to their native land, they should be at full liberty to do so; or if any of the people of Holland should desire to emigrate to the colony, the way should remain entirely open to them just as it always had been.

Farther Negotiations

Two or three days more were spent in negotiations between the governor and Colonel Nicoll. The governor had now, indeed, no rational hope of being able to save the colony, but he clung to the possibility, to the last, with the energy of a drowning man. His authority was yet acknowledged, nominally, in the town, but all effort, on the part of the people to prepare for defense, had been abandoned by them. Still the governor kept the Dutch flag flying from the fort, and seemed determined to defend it to the end.

Advance of the Ships of War

Things continued in this state until Thursday, and then Colonel Nicoll, finding that the negotiations were not likely to lead to anything but delay, determined to wait no longer. He accordingly sent to the shore at Long Island—a little below the site of Brooklyn—a body of troops, with orders to march to the East River, and to be ready there to cross over into the town, and then ordered the two principal

Fall of New Amsterdam.

ships to weigh anchor, and advance up the harbor, and take positions before the town, so as to present their broadsides to it, ready to open fire.

The governor, from the battlements of the fort, saw the ships approaching. In a fever of desperation and excitement, he ordered the men to their guns, brought the guns into the range of the approaching vessels, and was waiting for them to draw near enough to receive the fire—the gunners standing ready with the matches lighted—when a delegation from the people of the town, consisting of the two clergymen already mentioned, came in, and earnestly begged him to desist.

They entreated him, at any rate, not to be the first to fire. If blood must be shed, they implored him not to begin the contest, but to leave that dreadful responsibility to rest upon the enemy. By means of these earnest remonstrances, and, as some accounts say, by actually taking hold of him, and leading him away, they succeeded in preventing the fort from opening fire. The frigates, accordingly, advanced without opposition, and took their places before the town, while the governor went into the streets, and endeavored to rally the men, and induce them to make a stand against the enemy, so soon as they should attempt to land.

CONSTERNATION AMONG THE INHABITANTS

A new communication was sent to Colonel Nicoll, but he refused to listen to any farther parleying. He demanded that the white "flag of peace," as he called it—really the signal of surrender—should be hoisted upon the fort, otherwise he must proceed to "do his duty." He allowed them until the next day to consider the question.

This ultimatum produced the greatest consternation throughout the town. Many of the people came with their wives and children, and implored the governor to yield. But he said he would rather be carried a corpse to the grave than to surrender the place. Finally, the leading men drew up a formal memorial, addressed to the governor, and expressed in the most earnest and decided language, in which they remonstrated against the wickedness of exposing a population of fifteen hundred men, women, and children, to all the horrors attendant upon the bombardment and storming of a town, when there was not the smallest hope of making any effectual resistance.

This memorial was signed by all the principal inhabitants of the place, and then put into the governor's hands.

THE SURRENDER

The governor found himself, at last, compelled to yield. He saw very clearly that he could not succeed if he were to attempt to defend the town. The fort consisted only of earthworks, faced with a wooden stockade—having been built solely as a defense against Indians, and wholly insufficient to resist a cannonading from English ships of war. In the rear, the only defense was what remained of the wooden palisade which had been erected along the line of Wall Street, as was stated in a former chapter, and which was in a very decayed and dilapidated condition. The people of the town refused to fight, and he had, of course, no troops to depend upon except the garrison of the fort, who, though they did not sympathize with the people— being foreign troops provided by the West India Company—after all, felt no interest in the contest.

Seeing, therefore, that the case was utterly and absolutely hopeless, the governor, by the end of the week, brought his mind to the conviction that he must surrender. Articles of capitulation were accordingly drawn up, in which the rights and privileges of the Dutch inhabitants of the colony were all fully and carefully guarded. The terms were readily accepted by Colonel Nicoll. On Monday, the articles were formally ratified. The governor, at the head of his Dutch garrison, marched out of the town, with the honors of war, to a landing place at the foot of Beaver Street, where they all embarked on board a ship, and sailed for Holland.

Colonel Nicoll sent on shore a small force to take possession of the town. He changed the name of the colony from New Netherland, and of the town from New Amsterdam, to New York—in honor of the royal duke in whose name he was acting; and thus the group of settlements on the Hudson took its place among the other settlements on the coast, as one of the English colonies of North America.

CHAPTER X
GROWTH AND EXTENSION OF
THE COLONIES

The Three Great Centers

The settlements at Plymouth, at Massachusetts Bay, and at the mouth of the Hudson River—the origin and early history of which have been narrated in the preceding chapters—became, for all the northern part of the territory which now pertains to the United States, the three great centers of colonization, from which, by a gradual process of expansion and embranchment, nearly all the other colonies ultimately sprang. These new settlements spread themselves slowly along the sea coast, choosing, as they advanced, the points where land-locked bays, or the mouths of inlets, furnished places of security for shipping, and also into the interior, along the banks of the great rivers, such as the Merrimac, the Connecticut, and the Hudson. Some of these settlements were made by companies of adventurous men, who separated themselves amicably from the parent colonies to go in search of richer land, or wider scope. In other cases, divisions arose from religious or political differences of opinion, which led to the departure of disaffected portions of the community, and the establishment of new homes and new institutions, in some unoccupied part of the vast wilderness which was open to them.

First Knowledge of the Connecticut River

It is a curious circumstance, that the attention of the colonists was first called to the existence and the importance of the Connecticut River, by a delegation of Indians, who went to Boston within a very few years after the foundation of the Massachusetts colony, and actually invited the English to come and make a settlement there.

They offered them supplies of corn, and a certain number of beaver-skins, as an inducement. It proved, on inquiry, that the real motive of the Indians in making this offer, originated in the fact that they were afraid of the power of a neighboring tribe, their enemies, and they hoped to have the English for their allies, if they could induce them to make a settlement in their vicinity.

The Boston people thought it best to decline this proposal, but, two or three years afterward, some of the Plymouth colonists determined to establish a factory in that quarter, for trading with the Indians. So they framed a house, for this purpose, in Plymouth, and putting the timbers on board a vessel, they sailed to the Connecticut River, and went up as far as where the town of Hartford now stands, and there they found a company of Dutch traders, from New Amsterdam, in possession before them. This was very soon after the settlement at New Amsterdam was founded.

The Dutch on the Connecticut

The Dutchmen had built a fort, and had two cannons mounted upon it. The Plymouth men went on, expecting to be fired upon. They were allowed to pass, however, and, going farther up the river, they landed at last on the site of the present town of Windsor. There they put up their house, fortified it with palisades and guns, and, leaving a part of their company to buy skins of the Indians, and to guard the station, they went back down the river with their vessel.

The Dutch and the English continued both to claim the right to the valley of the Connecticut for many years after this, and quarrels and fights were continually occurring between them, for a long series of years, until at length, as related in the last chapter, the Dutch power on the whole continent was annihilated by the taking of New Netherland, in 1664, by the English, under Colonel Nicoll.

Emigration to the Connecticut from Massachusetts

Twenty or thirty years, however, before this conquest, and while both the Dutch and English held their trading stations on the river, a project was formed, by a number of quite influential persons who lived in several towns in the vicinity of Boston, to form a company for emigrating to the Connecticut, and establishing a permanent settlement there. This was in 1633. The leaders of this movement were Samuel Stone and Thomas Hooker, who were ministers of Newtown, and whose names are greatly celebrated in the history of Connecticut. Associated with them were a number of influential and prominent men in many of the neighboring towns. They had a great deal of difficulty in obtaining the consent of the government and people of the Massachusetts colony to their going. Finally, however, after spending one or two years in arguing and discussing the question, the obstacles were so far surmounted, that several companies of emigrants prepared for their departure. One of these expeditions consisted of sixty persons, men, women, and children. It was late in the fall when these expeditions set out. They traveled on foot, driving their cattle, their sheep, and their pigs before them. After long and painful journeys, these various parties arrived safely at their destination.

It was so late in the season, however, and the hardships and privations, which they endured were so great, that many of the people became discouraged—and, in the course of six weeks, a considerable number of them found their way back to Boston, having been ten days on the way. They arrived half frozen, half starved, and bringing dreadful accounts of the hardships and privations which they had encountered. One of their number had been drowned by breaking through the ice of a stream that they had been obliged to cross by the way.

Difficulty with the English Proprietors

Those who remained endured as well as they could the hardships and privations of the winter, and in the spring commenced the work of clearing land and making farms. They were soon joined by other emigrants—but their troubles were not yet ended, for very soon there came an agent from England, representing certain parties who held the patent for the country of the Connecticut, which had been conveyed to them by those to whom it had been granted by the king. This agent claimed, on the part of his principals, that the whole country belonged to them, and that all the emigrants who had established themselves in it were trespassers.

This difficulty was, however, in the end adjusted, and the people were allowed to remain on certain terms and conditions that were not unreasonable.

FINAL ESTABLISHMENT OF THE COLONY

The several companies, which made the journey to the valley of the Connecticut in the fall, were only considered as small parties sent forward in advance, who were to take possession of the ground, and prepare the way for the reception of the main body of emigrants, who were to defer their journey until the following summer. In the course of the winter, these last sold their property, and closed up their affairs; and, early in June, they all set out upon the journey. The ministers, Hooker and Stone, accompanied this expedition, which was much larger than those which preceded it. They traveled on foot, except that Mrs. Hooker, who was in feeble health, was borne upon a sort of bed, or litter, fastened upon the back of a horse. They had wagons, however, for the transportation of their household goods. There were, of course, no roads, and the company were obliged to make a way for themselves as they went along. They directed their course by the compass. When they came to forests, pioneers went forward with axes, to cut away the trees and underbrush, so as to make a passage for the wagons, and for the flocks and herds. When they came to rivers and streams too deep to be forded, they halted until rude but strong bridges could be built. They had tents to shelter a portion of the party, and the rest either bivouacked in the open air, or crept under the wagons if it rained. Their flocks and herds— they had a hundred and sixty head of cattle with them—gained their sustenance by stopping every day to graze, and to browse upon the young leaves of the forest; and the cows were milked regularly every morning and night, to supply the wants of the women and children.

Of course, they traveled very slowly. It took them a fortnight to accomplish what a single locomotive of the present day would have done for the whole company in five hours. I know of nothing which shows the progress of civilization, and the power of coal, as developed and applied at the present day, by means of steam, more strikingly than such a fact as this.

The journey, however, seems to have been not a disagreeable one to them. The season of the year was pleasant ; the country was beautiful, though solitary. The air was balmy, and the woods were full of blooming flowers and singing birds.

The arrival of this body of reinforcements placed the colony at once upon a sure and permanent footing. Other parties of emigrants followed, a regular government was organized, and the settlements were gradually extended up and down the river, until at length the whole valley was occupied by the villages and farms of the English immigrants.

The Colony of New Haven

Although the region of New Haven became subsequently united with the valley of the Connecticut to form the present state, the two districts were separately colonized, and they remained for a long time distinct. The colony of New Haven was founded in the spring of 1638. The Indian name of the harbor was Quinnipiack. The persons who first conceived the idea of making a settlement in this place, were Theophilus Eaton, a gentleman from England of wealth and of fervent piety, and his minister, John Davenport, who had both recently come to America. These men had formed the opinion that the scriptures contained a complete system, not only of moral duty, but, also, of civil government and law, and they conceived the design of establishing a colony based upon the Bible alone.

After much inquiry, they made choice of the Bay of Quinnipiack as the place for their settlement.

The party that they took with them was very small. The voyage from Boston occupied a fortnight. The company spent the first Sabbath, after they landed, under the shelter of an oak, where the minister preached a sermon on the leading of Jesus into the wilderness to be tempted of the devil—rather a sinister subject of discourse, one would think, considering the circumstances of the congregation. Very soon they drew up articles of association, which

157

they called their Plantation Covenant, in which they agreed that their whole system of government, and all the regulations and laws of the community, should be drawn from the Scriptures alone.

It would be very interesting, if our space would allow, to follow the history of this colony a little way, and give an account of the progress they made, and the difficulties which they encountered, in carrying out their design. It is sufficient, however, to say, that the original idea, on which the enterprise had been founded, began very soon to be essentially modified in practice, and, finally, was abandoned altogether. The settlement itself prospered, however, and very soon became one of the most important colonies on the continent.

Rhode Island

All the companies of settlers, above described, in branching off from the central colonies, effected their separation in the end in an amicable manner, though, in some cases, not without considerable preliminary discussion, and even opposition. The founding of the colony of Rhode Island, on the other hand, was the result of a long continued political and religious dissension, which ended finally in an open quarrel.

An Impracticable Man

The leading person in these transactions was the famous Roger Williams. He was a young minister of uncommon talent and great energy of character, and was one of those men who follow out, in the most stern and uncompromising manner, their own theoretical ideas of right and wrong, in respect both to the institutions of society, and to the common affairs of life, and thus often occasion a vast amount of dissension and trouble. In doing this, they shelter themselves under the example of Jesus Christ, who came, they remember, not to send peace on earth, but the sword.

Roger Williams emigrated from Europe in 1631, and went immediately to Salem. Here his talents and his originality attracted attention, and he was chosen pastor of one of the churches; but he soon began to advance such doctrines as to throw the community into a great state of excitement. He insisted on the churches coming out with a formal and public expression of their repentance of the sin of having, in former years, when they were in England, and before their separation from the English church, been connected with that idolatrous system of worship, and thus implicated in the guilt of it. It was not enough to have forsaken that communion. He called for a public and solemn denunciation and renouncement of it, as an act of penitence.

He maintained that the civil magistrate had no authority to enforce what was called the first table of the Decalogue, which comprised offenses against God alone, and so the laws against Sabbath-breaking and blasphemy were acts of usurpation, and were null and void. He made great difficulty about the practice of forming associations of ministers for mutual conference and prayer, denouncing such associations in the most determined manner, as containing the germs of future ecclesiastical hierarchies. He maintained that all titles to land in the colonies, held by grant from English proprietors, were null, as the land belonged to the Indians alone, and, unless held by conveyance from them, no man was the owner of his farm.

He became engaged in a very earnest controversy on the question of whether women ought, or ought not to, wear veils in the churches. He maintained that the cross on the English flag was an idolatrous symbol, and insisted that it should be taken out of the colors of the regiments of soldiers. He declared that it was a sin for any magistrate to administer an oath to an unregenerate person—for an oath was a religious act, and, by administering it, the magistrate held communion with a wicked man, in the worship of God, and caused him to take the name of God in vain. He called on his own church to renounce fellowship with all the other churches, because they persisted in what he had thus shown to be sinful; and when they would not do it, he renounced fellowship with them; and not being able to induce his wife to follow his example in this respect, he renounced fellowship with her, by refusing to join with her in family prayers, or in asking a blessing at the table!

REDEEMING TRAITS OF ROGER WILLIAMS' CHARACTER

Notwithstanding all this, however, Roger Williams was possessed of many great and noble traits of character. He was conscientious, faithful, fearless, uncompromising in respect to all questions in which he considered the principles of right and wrong were involved, and, so far as can be seen, wholly disinterested and unselfish in all that he did. He was a man of commanding eloquence, and of great power in respect to the personal ascendancy which he acquired over his followers. He acted under the influence of a certain exaltation of spirit, which—if instead of having been expended on formalities of no real and present importance, whatever future consequences his excited imagination may have seen looming from them in the future, had been exercised on really grand and momentous truths, and upon some wide and conspicuous field of action—would have made him one of the greatest men of the age.

SENTENCE OF BANISHMENT

Of course, the earnest inculcation of such doctrines as Roger Williams advocated made great difficulty. For three or four years, the churches of Boston, Salem, and Plymouth, in all of which places he preached, and urged his views, and obtained followers, were kept in a state of continual turmoil. The governments were repeatedly called upon to interpose in the various quarrels and dissensions which arose. At last, the author of all the mischief was brought to a kind of trial, before the General Court, and was condemned to be banished from the colony. He was allowed six weeks to prepare for his departure, and if he did not go before the expiration of that time, the magistrates were authorized to send him away themselves, wherever they pleased.

FLIGHT

It was in September that this decree was passed; and as, at the expiration of the allotted period, winter would be approaching, the time was afterward extended to the spring. Roger Williams, in the meantime, began to form a plan for establishing a settlement of his own, somewhere on the shores of Narragansett Bay. While he was busied about his preliminary arrangements, the government came to the conclusion that they would not like to have him so near. They secretly determined, therefore, to seize him, put him on board an English ship, and send him to England. Roger Williams, in some way or other, heard of this plan in time to frustrate it. When the officer, who was to arrest him, came to Salem for the purpose, he found that his intended prisoner had escaped. He had left his family three days before, and had fled for refuge into the woods, although it was now midwinter.

The unhappy exile wandered about all winter, seeking the hospitality and protection of savages, who were almost as houseless and destitute as himself. "For fourteen weeks, during this bitter winter season," he says, "I was sorely tossed about, not knowing what bread or bed did mean." The Indians were, however, very friendly to him—his power of gaining a personal ascendancy over all who came into communication with him, being the same, it would seem, with savages as with civilized men.

Final Settlement in Rhode Island

In the spring he found his way to the River Seekonk, a small stream which flows into Narragansett Bay, on the Massachusetts side. Here some of his more devoted friends and partisans from Salem came and joined him; and they began to clear the land, and to commence the work of making farms. But very soon Mr. Williams received a letter from the governor of the Plymouth colony, saying that the place which he had chosen was within their limits, and though they had themselves no objection to his remaining there, it might possibly make difficulty between them and "the Bay," as the Massachusetts colony was designated, if he were allowed to establish himself there without any remonstrance on their part. The governor, therefore, courteously suggested to him that he should cross the water to the western side, where he would be beyond the limits of both colonies, and would be entirely free.

Mr. Williams at once acceded to this request, and his readiness to do so shows that he was, by no means, so tenacious of his ground in cases where only his own rights and interests were concerned, as in those which he imagined involved some moral principle.

So the little company abandoned the clearings which they had begun, and, embarking in a canoe, six in all, they went down the river, and over to the western side, looking for a new site. They chose at last the place where the city of Providence now stands. Mr. Williams bought a tract of land of the Indian's, raising the funds to pay for it by a mortgage of the property which he had left in Salem. Many families, consisting of persons who had sympathized with him in his previous conflicts and trials, came to join his settlement, which rapidly increased and extended, until it became the colony of Rhode Island.

The French in Acadia

In the course of the first twenty or thirty years after the establishment of the Plymouth and Massachusetts Bay colonies, many subordinate settlements were formed to the northward, in the direction of the territory now occupied by the states of Vermont and New Hampshire, and several trading stations were established at the mouths of the rivers in Maine. Here, however, the English colonists came into collision with the French, who had commenced settlements in Canada, and who claimed a large part of what is now Maine, under the name of Acadia. Many difficulties arose out of this conflict, and these, together with the rigor of the climate, retarded the settlement of the country very much, though the long duration and severe cold of the winters made the furs more valuable, and greatly excited the competition for the Indian trade. It was long, however, before any permanent settlements were established in these regions.

The Central Colonies

The circumstances, under which the settlement of the territory of Pennsylvania, of Delaware, and of Maryland was first commenced, were very peculiar, differing in all respects from those attending the early history of the other colonies—but they cannot be narrated here.

Conclusion

We have thus, in the present work, endeavored to present to the reader an account, as full as our limits will allow, of the origin and early history of the principal Northern Colonies, as separate and distinct communities. The nature and the occasion of the several alliances and confederations which they formed among themselves, and with their sister communities toward the south, and the different wars in which they were engaged, while they continued in the colonial state, will be narrated in the next volume of this series.

The End.

Lightning Source UK Ltd.
Milton Keynes UK
UKHW021928270123
416101UK00006B/140